On Saturday, 29 August 1942, four Tiger I tanks of schwere Panzer-Abteilung 502, led by the battalion commander Major Richard Märker, made their way through the dense, marshy forests south-east of Leningrad, modern-day St Petersburg, towards the German defensive line. Days earlier a Soviet attack had created a large bulge in the front between Sinyavino and the village of Gaitolovo and Major Märker had been ordered to support the infantry units in the area. These four Tigers made up the battalion's total complement of heavy vehicles at the time and Märker protested vigorously that the employment of his tanks in such small numbers, in terrain that could not have been more unfavourable, would negate any advantage these powerful new vehicles may have enjoyed, including the element of surprise.

But Hitler had insisted that the Tigers be sent into action as soon as possible, confident that the heavy Panzers would tip the balance in favour of the German units besieging Leningrad which he regarded as the birthplace of Bolshevism. Little or no thought had been given to the most basic logistical requirements and Major Märker's men had been allowed just nine days to familiarise themselves with their new tanks. The battalion had no recovery vehicles or even spare parts.

By the end of the day not a single shot had been fired in anger and three of the four Tigers had been immobilised by mechanical failures. Although all three vehicles were later salvaged, the battalion would not be ready to take part in any further operations for almost a month. The first action of what was to become one of the legendary weapons systems of the Second World War could not have been more inauspicious.

This book is the seventh in the T... series dealing with the Tiger I and ... tanks and completes the story by ... on the first vehicles to leave the pr... line and go into battle during late ... addition, it examines the evolution of the heavy Panzer units which fought on the Eastern Front up to the spring of 1943 (1).

The failure of Operation Barbarossa to end the war in 1941 meant that new ways had to be found to defeat the Soviet Union and by the beginning of 1942 plans were well underway to equip the army with a new heavy tank and the development of what was to become the Tiger I is covered in the Technical Details and Modifications section. Other aspects were also subject to change including vehicle camouflage and this is also considered. I hope that a thorough examination of the matter, beginning as it does in the pre-war period, will give a greater appreciation of the colour schemes adopted, often unofficially, during the summer of 1942 which eventually led to the institution of the Dunkelgelb, or dark yellow, base colour with which I am sure most readers will be familiar.

Less than 100 Tiger tanks took part in the battles around Leningrad and the attacks to recapture Kharkov, the principal actions covered by this book, and the available photographs were often taken under atrocious conditions and sometimes at great risk. These factors go some way towards explaining the mediocre quality of some of the images reproduced in this book but I have decided to include a number as they are directly relevant to the units and vehicles described. The lack of clarity in some photographs has also led to a certain amount of speculation on my part in the creation of the illustrations but where this has occurred I have tried to make it clear.

1943.

An early production Tiger I of 8.Kompanie, SS-Panzer-Regiment 2 photographed in the streets of Kharkov in March 1943. The company's ten Tigers were all assembled in December 1942 and points to note here are the toolbox and 15-ton jack on the hull rear plate, the metal exhaust covers and S-mine dischargers. Just visible above the toolbox is the regiment's unit insignia. The trackguards, both with triangular end sections, have been removed and placed on the engine deck. Note also the large stowage box which partly covers the pistol port and was a common feature of this company's tanks. The 20-litre fuel containers, or Wehrmacht Einheitskanister, behind the stowage box are probably painted in Dunkelgrau RAL 7021

Eastern Europe 1942-1943

FINLAND

Helsinki

Gulf of Finland

Lake Ladoga

Tallinn

ESTONIA

Kohta-Järve

LENINGRAD (St Petersburg)

Gatchina

Pärnu

Tartu

Novgorod

Ustyuzhna

Baltic Sea

Ventspils

Pskov

Staraya Russa

Rybinsk

Demyansk

Riga

Kholm

Kalinin

Jelgava

Ostrov

Velikiye Luki

Memel

LATVIA

Rzhev

MOSCOW

LITHUANIA

Daugavpils

Kolomna

Königsberg (Kaliningrad)

Kaunus

Vitebsk

Yartsevo

Vyazma

Serpukhov

Vilna (Vilnius)

EAST PRUSSIA

Orsha

Smolensk

Kaluga

Ryazan

GERMANY

Bialystok

Minsk

BYELORUSSIA

Tula

WARSAW

Baranowicze

Mogilev

Kaluga

Siedlce

Bobriusk

Bryansk

Orel

Brest-Litovsk

Klintsy

Lublin

Pinsk

Gomel

Yelets

POLAND (GENERAL GOVERNMENT)

Mozyr

Shostka

Kovel

Kursk

Voronezh

Lutsk

Novohrad-Volynskyi

Nezhin

Konotop

Jaroslaw

Brody

Zhytomyr

Kiev

Sumy

Romny

Belgorod

Lvov

Pavlovsk

Ternopol

Berdychiv

UKRAINE

Cherkasy

Kharkov

Khmelnytskyi

Poltava

Zmie

Vinnytsia

Kremenchug

Kropyvnytskyi

Dniepropetrovsk

Pervomaisk

Krivoy Rog (Kryvyi Rih)

Stalino (Donetsk)

Nikopol

Zaporozhye

Nikolayev

Rostov-on-Don

Kherson

Mariupol

Krasnoperekopsk

Black Sea

Sea of Azov

Simferopol

Kerch

Sevastopol

Kursk

Voronezh

Belgorod

Kharkov

Serafimovich

Krasnograd

Millerovo

Stalingrad

Kalch

Stalino

Kamensk-Shakhlinski

Zaporozhye

Rostov-on-Don

Bataysk

Astrakan

Pavlovskaya

Salsk

Elitsa

Kerch

Tikhoretsk

Taman

Armavir

Maykop

Mozduk

Taupse

Nizhniy Kurp

Grozny

Black Sea

Beslan

The map at left depicts Eastern Europe with national borders as they were in June 1941 when the invasion of the Soviet Union began. The front in what is today the Baltic States, northern Russia, Belarus and northern Ukraine remained relatively static for much of 1942. As a result of the German efforts to push towards the oil fields of the Caucasus region, codenamed Fall Blau or Case Blue, the focus of operations for much of the year shifted to the vast expanse of land between the present-day Georgian frontier and Stalingrad on the Volga River and this area is shown in the small inset map. Limited assaults around Leningrad, modern St Petersburg, and in the sector of Heeresgruppe Mitte were designed to draw the Russians away from the southern front. The broken line in both maps indicates the front as it was in mid-November 1942, just prior to the launch of the Red Army's offensive to cut off Stalingrad, and the shaded area in the large map denotes territory recaptured by the Soviets up to early February 1943. The timeline presented below details the events that occurred between August 1942, when the first Tigers arrived on the Eastern Front, and March 1943 when the events chronicled in *TankCraft 20, Tiger I: German Army Heavy Tank Eastern Front, Summer 1943* begin.

1 August 1942. As part of Fall Blau, the divisions of Heeresgruppe A continue to push into the Caucasus region, reaching the Kuban River on this day. Further to the north, the Soviet defenders of Kalach in the bend of the Don River to the west Stalingrad, are completely surrounded.

4 August 1942. Elements of 4.Panzerarmee cross the Aksay River, a tributary of the Don which runs into the Tsimlyansk Reservoir west of Stalingrad.

5 August 1942. The tanks of 1.Panzerarmee capture Voroshilovsk, over 200 miles to the south-east of Rostov and on the following day cross the Kuban River at Armavir.

7 August 1942. Units of 6.Armee cross the Don River at Kalach and drive towards the Volga and Stalingrad.

9 August 1942. The tanks of 1.Panzeramee reach the Maikop oilfields only to find them in flames. Elsewhere, 1.Panzerarmee reaches Krasnodar on the Kuban River.

10 August 1942. Units of 6.Armee reach the Volga River and bring Stalingrad under artillery fire.

12 August 1942. Pushing towards the Grozny oilfields, units of Heeresgruppe A capture Elista near the coast of the Caspian Sea.

14 August 1942. German forces cross the upper Kuban River at Krasnodar. On the following day advance elements of Heeresgruppe A reach the foothills of the Caucasus Mountains.

19 August 1942. The divisions of 6.Armee begin attacks on the city of Stalingrad.

20 August 1942. Despite determined Russian counterattacks to the north of Stalingrad, the German troops fight their way through to the banks of the Volga. An attack from Abganerovo towards Tundutovo, about 60 kilometres south of Stalingrad, made by the tanks of XXXXVIII.Panzerkorps is unable to break the Soviet defences. Russian resistance, which had been half-hearted along the Don River front is now nothing short of fanatical.

22 August 1942. Further south, the advance towards the Black Sea port of Suchumi, modern-day Sokhumi in Georgia, bogs down.

23 August 1942. The four serviceable Tigers of schwere Panzer-Abteilung (sPz Abt) 502, together with a number of Pzkpfw III tanks and parts of the battalion's Werkstatt-Kompanie, leave Hanover for the Eastern Front. On the same day, Hitler orders the destruction of Leningrad. The Luftwaffe begins a 48-hour bombing campaign against Stalingrad that reduces the city to a sea of flames. The tanks of 4.Panzerarmee, which had been ordered to swing north to support the German units fighting in Stalingrad, are held up by stiff resistance at Tinguta, some 40 kilometres from the city centre. Men of 1.Gebirgs-Division raise the German national flag on Mount Elbrus, the highest peak in the Caucasus mountain range.

25 August 1942. The attacks conducted by 4.Panzerarmee south of Stalingrad come to a standstill.

29 August 1942. The tanks of sPz Abt 502 arrive at the front near Mga, a small town on a tributary of the Neva River east of Leningrad, and are ordered to take up positions in the German defensive line. Three of the four Tigers break down before they can reach their objective.

This initial production Tiger I was one of the first ten vehicles to leave the assembly lines and the first Tiger to be captured by the Soviets. This tank is also shown on page 17 of the Camouflage & Markings section of this book.

1 September 1942. Advance German units reach the Black Sea coast in the Caucasus while the tanks of 1.Panzerarmee cross the Terek River at Mozduk in present-day North Ossetia.

3 September 1942. Units of 6.Armee and 4.Panzerarmee meet west of Stalingrad near the village of Pitomnik.

6 September 1942. The Russian naval base of Novorossiysk on the Black Sea falls to the men of 4.Gebirgs-Division. Heavy fighting is underway in the suburbs of Stalingrad and on the following day German units push through the city to reach the banks of the Volga.

9 September 1942. Impatient with Generalfeldmarschall List's lack of success in his drive towards Astrakhan and Baku, Hitler sacks him and assumes direct command of Heeresgruppe A.

13 September 1942. At Stalingrad, the units of 6.Armee begin a massive assault to secure the city. Although the Soviet perimeter is reduced a narrow strip along the Volga, the Germans are unable to break the Russian resistance. General Paulus, the commander of 6.Armee, appeals to Hitler for substantial reinforcements and raises concerns about the defence of the German flanks which has been left to Italian, Hungarian and Romanian units.

22 September 1942. The southern half of Stalingrad and the Volga landing is in German hands and a Soviet counterattack on the following day is held off. During an attack in support of 170.Infanterie-Division near Tortolovo on the Leningrad Front the four Tigers of sPz Abt 502 are all bogged down in the marshy terrain. Although three are later recovered, the fourth is under constant enemy fire and cannot be reached.

24 September 1942. In the Caucasus, units of Heeresgruppe A launch an attack against the Black Sea port of Tuapse. After days of heavy fighting the Germans secure the Mamayev Hill outside Stalingrad. In the city, the Russians are pushed out of the Red October and Barricades factories and neighbouring housing estates.

30 September 1942. The commander of sPz Abt 502 reports that nine serviceable Tigers and twenty-five Pzkpfw III tanks are on hand. The battalion is moved to Tosno, a small village about 45 kilometres south of Leningrad.

4 October 1942. The fourth major attempt to secure the city of Stalingrad begins as the tanks of XIV.Panzerkorps are hurled at the Dzerzhinskiy Tractor factory in the city's northern suburbs.

6 October 1942. The tanks of III.Panzerkorps capture Malgobek at the bend of the Terek river in the Caucasus.

15 October 1942. Two new Tigers, shipped from Paderborn for sPz Abt 502, arrive at Gory, south-east of Leningrad at the confluence of the Mga and Voytolovka Rivers.

29 October 1942. German units capture Nalchik in the Caucasus, less than 129 kilometres from the oil fields of Grozny. Progress in Stalingrad is by now measured by the capture of streets or even houses, usually at great loss.

2 November 1942. The tanks of 13.Panzer-Division are held up outside Ordzhonikidze on the Terek River in modern-day Dagestan, the furthest point reached by any German unit in the Soviet Union. Within days the division is struggling to escape encirclement.

11 November 1942. In Stalingrad the Germans secure a 600-metre sector along the bank of the Volga near the Red October factory.

19 November 1942. The Red Army launches major assaults to the north and south of Stalingrad. German attempts to bolster the Romanian units on the western and southern edges of the front by hastily-formed Kampfgruppen are unable to stop the Russian advance towards Kalach on the Don River. The records of sPz Abt 503 state that on this day the Tigers were modified for hot-climate employment although what this means exactly is not clear.

21 November 1942. The commander of sPz Abt 502, Major Richard Märker, is summoned to Hitler's headquarters and replaced by Hauptmann Artur Wollschläger. On the following day Soviet units take Kalach, completing the encirclement of 4.Panzerarmee and 6.Armee.

23 November 1942. The first three Tigers of sPz Abt 501 arrive in North Africa.

25 November 1942. The crews of sPz Abt 502 are finally able to destroy the Tiger that had become bogged down during the attack on Tortolov in late September. During November the battalion's second company is formed at Paderborn in Germany from elements of Panzer-Regiment 1 and Panzer-Regiment 35.

26 November 1942. On the southern front, the Germans are pushed back to the west bank of the Don River.

27 November 1942. Heeresgruppe Don, commanded by Generalfeldmarschall von Manstein, is formed specifically for the relief of Stalingrad.

3 December 1942. Heeresgruppe Don is reinforced by a number of divisions transferred from the West. Manstein resists the temptation to attack prematurely although Hitler constantly insists that the relief operation begin immediately.

12 December 1942. The units of Heeresgruppe Don, including three Panzer divisions, launch an attack towards the south of Stalingrad precipitating a three-day tank battle.

16 December 1942. The commander of sPz Abt 503 reports that the battalion's twenty Tiger I tanks are modified for deployment to the East. The exact significance of this statement is not clear and it may have meant that the tanks were repainted or that the Feifel air cleaning systems were removed. In the Caucasus the Red Army begins an offensive aimed at cutting off Rostov-on-Don.

19 December 1942. The tanks of Heeresgruppe Don are only 50 kilometres from the centre of Stalingrad but Hitler forbids any attempt by the garrison to break out.

21 December 1942. The tanks of sPz Abt 503 begin leaving Germany for the Eastern Front.

23 December 1942. Manstein's tanks reach the banks of the Myshkova River, south-west of Stalingrad, but can go no further. The units of Heeresgruppe Don are exhausted and begin to withdraw towards Kotelnikovo, the starting point of the operation.

27 December 1942. Hitler agrees to allow the divisions of Heeresgruppe A and Heeresgruppe Don to withdraw to a defensive line almost 200 kilometres west of Stalingrad, effectively abandoning the men of 6.Armee to their fate.

29 December 1942. With four Tigers and five Pzkpfw III tanks, 2.Kompanie, sPz Abt 502 arrives on the Eastern Front. The tanks are subordinated to Heeresgruppe Don and do not join 1.Kompanie which was still on the northern sector of the front.

1 January 1943. The Tigers of sPz Abt 503 are deployed at the Manych River bridge, south-east of Rostov-on-Don, to cover the Axis forces withdrawing from the Caucasus.

5 January 1943. 2.Kompanie, sPz Abt 503 holds up a Russian attack aimed at Stavropol but is forced to retreat under cover of darkness, abandoning the town to the Soviets. The following day both companies counterattack and drive the Red Army units out of Stavropol and back towards modern-day Nevinnomyssk. The tanks of 2.Kompanie, sPz Abt 502 arrive at Proletarskaya, about 150 kilometres south-east of Rostov-on-Don.

By the first weeks of February 1943, 1.Kompanie, schwere Panzer-Abteilung 502 had been reduced to so few tanks that the three-digit company numbering system was abandoned and the five surviving Tigers were simply numbered consecutively as can be seen here. The numbers varied slightly in style but most were placed at the centre of the turret sides and rendered in black.

7 January 1943. From Proletarskaya, 2.Kompanie, sPz Abt 502 is redirected to the area around Kuberle and, almost unbelievably, completes the road march without a single mechanical failure.

9 January 1943. After three attempts, the Tigers of sPz Abt 503, supported by the infantry of Panzergrenadier-Regiment 128, fail to break the Russian lines near present-day Veseloye and withdraw to Proletarskaya.

10 January 1943. In a fierce firefight near Budenovskaya, on the eastern bank of the Manych River, Tiger number 231 of sPz Abt 503 commanded by Leutnant Friedrich Zabel sustains over 250 hits from Russian tank and anti-tank weapons but stays in the fight. This vehicle is shown and discussed on page 24 of the Camouflage & Markings section of this book.

13 January 1943. 2.Kompanie, sPz Abt 503 and Sturmgeschütz-Abteilung 243, as part of Kampfgruppe Rossmann, undertake a counterattack between Novy Manych and Baraniki. But by the following day the Tigers had failed to negotiate the Yegorlyk River and only the light tanks managed to reach Baraniki. During the night Kampfgruppe Rossmann withdraws to Proletarskaya and the battalion is reunited.

16 January 1943. The Soviets complete the encirclement of Schlüsselburg, modern-day Shlisselburg, at the mouth of the Neva River.

17 January 1943. The Germans prepare to abandon Proletarskaya.

18 January 1943. In Schlüsselburg the remaining tanks of sPz Abt 502 attempt to break out towards Sinjavino. By the end of the day four Pzkpfw III tanks and five Tigers have been lost including Tiger number 100 which was captured intact by the Russian. The latter is shown in the Camouflage & Markings section on page 17.

21 January 1943. The surviving tanks of sPz Abt 503 arrive in Bataisk and begin crossing the Don River into Rostov on the following morning. On the same day the Tigers of 2.Kompanie, sPz Abt 502 are integrated into sPz Abt 503 as the battalion's third company.

2 February 1943. Encircled since late November 1942, the remnants of 6.Armee, holding out on the northern edge of Stalingrad, surrender to the Soviets. On the same day the last of the Tigers of 8.Kompanie, SS-Panzer-Regiment 2 arrive in the East and are unloaded at Kharkov.

4 February 1943. The last operational Pzkpfw III tank of sPz Abt 502 is destroyed in the fighting around Sinjavino, about 5 kilometres outside Schlüsselburg and 30 kilometres east of Leningrad on the shores of Lake Ladoga.

8 February 1943. Red Army units take Kursk, an important road and rail junction between Voronezh and Kiev, and continue their advance. On the same day the commander of 8.Kompanie, SS-Panzer-Regiment 2, Hauptsturmführer Rolf Grader, is killed as his Tigers defend the railway station at Kharkov.

9 February 1943. Soviet troops enter Belgorod, near the present-day Ukrainian border. The last vehicles of 13.Kompanie, SS-Panzer-Regiment 1 are unloaded at Kharkov. Under the command of Untersturmführer Michael Wittmann, and made up of three Tigers and five Pzkpfw III tanks, this group is diverted to Poltava and will not rejoin the company until early March.

10 February 1943. On the northern outskirts of Rostov, the tanks of sPz Abt 503 support attacks on Nishne-Ginlowskaja and around Sapadnyj railway station, where the fighting lasts for four days. But due to the confused nature of these operations the battalion is almost completely dispersed and by the next day some tanks are defending the suburbs of Rostov-on-Don. The tanks of 9.Kompanie, SS-Panzer-Regiment 3 leave Germany for the Eastern Front.

11 February 1943. The Tigers of 13.Kompanie, SS-Panzer-Regiment 1 go into action for the first time at Merefa, 15 kilometres south-west of Kharkov. Three Tigers of sPz Abt 502, under the command of Leutnant Herbert Meyer, destroy thirty-two Russian tanks in a single action near Mischkino, south-east of Leningrad.

12 February 1943. German troops evacuate Krasnodar and withdraw to the defensive positions in the Kuban bridgehead. On the same day 13.Kompanie, SS-Panzer-Regiment 1 suffers its first casualty when the tank of Unterscharführer Aus der Wischen catches fire during the road march to Poltava.

14 February 1943. Rostov-on-Don is captured by the Russians.

16 February 1943. Russian troops occupy parts of Kharkov, in modern-day Ukraine, after nine days of savage house-to-house fighting. On the same day the first tanks of 9.Kompanie, SS-Panzer-Regiment 3 are unloaded at the Poltava railway yard.

17 February 1943. The first Tigers of 13.Kompanie, Panzer-Regiment Grossdeutschland, under the command of Hauptmann Kraft-Helmuth Wallroth, arrive in the East.

18 February 1943. Hitler visits the headquarters of Heeresgruppe Süd at Zaporozhye to be informed that Kharkov, less than 200 kilometres to the north, has been abandoned to the Soviets.

21 February 1943. A German counterattack, aimed at retaking Kharkov, commences. The Tigers of 9.Kompanie, SS-Panzer-Regiment 3 see their first combat near Pavlograd.

22 February 1943. The tanks of sPz Abt 503 push back a massed frontal assault at the Sarmatskaya Balka, near the present-day Ukrainian border, claiming the destruction of a number of Russian tanks and anti-tank guns. After this the battalion is withdrawn to Taganrog and remains there for almost six weeks. On the same day Hauptsturmführer Karl Kloskowski, a platoon commander of 8.Kompanie, SS-Panzer-Regiment 2, captures and holds the bridge on the western edge of Pavlograd giving the Germans access to the town. Units of Heeresgruppe Mitte launch a limited counterattack in the area between the Dnieper and Donets rivers.

25 February 1943. The Red Army launches a major offensive against the front of Heeresgruppe Mitte.

1 March 1943. A Russian offensive to the south of Leningrad pushes the Germans towards the west. The evacuation of the pocket formed around Rzhev commences. Within two days the Russians capture the town.

7 March 1943. After almost two weeks of bitter fighting the Russian assault against Heeresgruppe Mitte is called off and the Soviet units are redirected towards the German drive on Kharkov. The tanks of 13.Kompanie, Panzer-Regiment Grossdeutschland go into action for the first time, attached to Kampfgruppe von Strachwitz.

8 March 1943. Four Tigers of 8.Kompanie, SS-Panzer-Regiment 2 capture the town of Valky, clearing the way for an assault on Kharkov.

11 March 1943. Supported by the Tigers of 13.Kompanie, SS-Panzer-Regiment 1, troops of SS-Panzergrenadier-Division Leibstandarte SS Adolf Hitler (LSSAH) fight their way into the centre of Kharkov. By the evening none of the company's tanks are operational.

12 March 1943. German troops evacuate Vyazma on the Moscow to Smolensk highway.

14 March 1943. The Germans declare that Kharkov has been secured although sporadic fighting continues for two more days. Both sides are exhausted by the ceaseless combat and at about this time the spring rains commence, greatly impeding mobile operations. The German counterattack has been a spectacular tactical success but a large bulge has been created in the front around Kursk which extends deep into the German lines.

19 March 1943. The Second Battle of Lake Ladoga begins with a major Soviet offensive launched between Kolpino and Krassny Bor, just 15 kilometres from the centre of Leningrad. The four serviceable Tigers of sPz Abt 502 manage to hold their positions and claim the destruction of forty enemy tanks over the next three days. The commander of 9.Kompanie, SS-Panzer-Regiment 3, Hauptsturmführer Alois Mooslechner, is killed when a faulty 8.8cm round explodes inside the turret of his Tiger.

21 March 1943. After two weeks of heavy fighting, Panzer-Regiment Grossdeutschland reports that none of the regiment's Tigers are operational.

22 March 1943. German troops recapture Belgorod.

29 March 1943. Oberfeldwebel Johannes Bölter of sPz Abt 502 is awarded the German Cross in Gold, one of only three soldiers of the battalion to receive the medal. The commander of 8.Kompanie, SS-Panzer-Regiment 2, Hauptsturmführer Friedrich Herzig, is relieved of duty and transferred to a training unit in Berlin.

31 March 1943. Five replacement crews for sPz Abt 503, accompanied by the battalion's Feldwebel Hans Fendesack, arrive in Taganrog. These men had all been in training for deployment in North Africa but had volunteered to fight in the East in order to stay together. Training at Ghent in Belgium, sPz Abt 505 reports that sixteen Tigers and twenty-three Pzkpfw III tanks are on hand. The complete battalion finally arrives on the Eastern Front during the first week of May. Two Tigers of sPz Abt 502, bogged down in the marshy ground around Tschernyschewo, are destroyed by their crews leaving the battalion with seven serviceable tanks. The commander of SS-Panzer-Regiment 1 reports that just five Tigers are operational

An early production Tiger I of 1.Kompanie, schwere Panzer-Abteilung 503 photographed during the fighting around Rostov-on-Don. Note the very dark background of the company number. This vehicle is also shown and discussed on page 22 of the Camouflage & Markings section of this book.

All units of the German Army were organised using detailed tables of establishment known as Kriegsstärkenachweisung, usually abbreviated to KstN. These lists gave the full personnel and equipment allowance for a particular unit and were referred to by a number and date. The latter was all-important as some numbers were duplicated. Raised in May 1942, the first three Tiger battalions were initially created using KstN 1150b Stabskompanie einer schweren Panzer-Abteilung, for the battalion headquarters, and KstN 1176 schwere Panzer-Kompanie for the tank companies, both dated 25 April 1942. At this time it was expected that schwere Panzer-Abteilungen 501 and 503 would be equipped with the Porsche design for the new tank, which was then under development, and sent to North Africa. An order of 21 August 1942 directed that schwere Panzer-Abteilungen 502 and 503 were to be reorganised according to KstN 1150d and KstN 1176d for the headquarters and tank companies respectively. These orders still allowed for either the Henschel or Porsche model. As both battalions received their Tigers at, or after, the time the order was disseminated we can be reasonably sure that this organisation was employed. In October 1942, schwere Panzer-Abteilung 501 was also ordered to be reorganised using the August tables. Each battalion was made up of two companies and contained twenty Tiger I and twenty-six Pzkpfw III light tanks. But this was, of course, the ideal and the true numbers fielded by each formation are given in the individual unit histories on the following pages.

SCHWERE PANZER-ABTEILUNG, AUGUST 1942

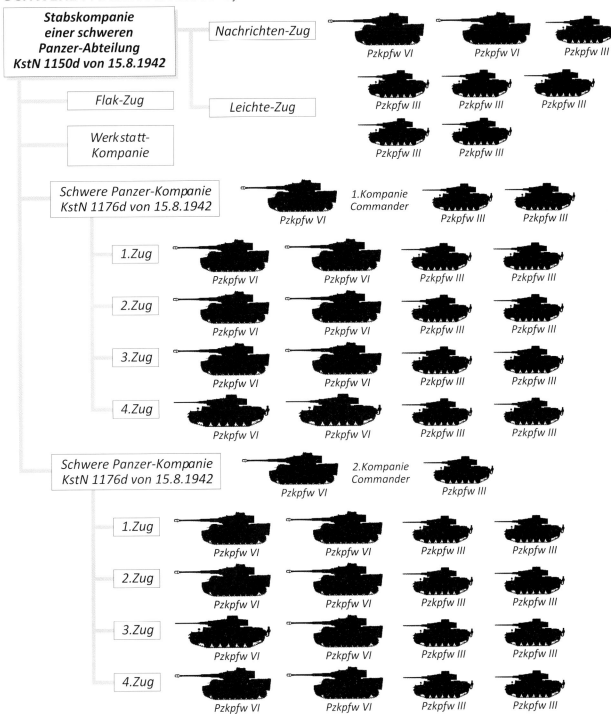

Note that although the version of light tank was specified as Pzkpfw III (5cm) in both KstN 1150d and KstN 1176d, numbers of the Pzkpfw III ausf N tank, 7.5cm weapon, were allocated as they became available.

When the Oberkommando des Heeres (OKH), the high command of the German Army, considered how the new heavy tanks would be employed it was originally intended that company-sized units of twenty vehicles be attached to Panzer divisions and employed as spearhead formations. These companies would be made up of Tigers and light tanks which were capable of performing duties for which the Tigers were unsuitable. The first units, schwere Panzer-Kompanien 501 and 502, were formed in February 1942 but by the following May both companies had been used to form schwere Panzer-Abteilung 501. By this time it had been decided that the Tigers would be best employed in battalion-sized units operating under army or corps-level command. The idea of providing the Panzer divisions with an organic Tiger unit was briefly revived during the first months of 1943 and the battalions that had been formed were attached to Panzer regiments where they were considered a third Abteilung, albeit on a semi-official basis. It was only after protests from the battalion commanders that the Tiger units reverted to their independent status.

The first battalions were organised in accordance with orders issued on 25 April 1942 and it should be remembered that at that time it was still expected that a number of Porsche-designed Tigers would be employed. An OKH order of 21 August directed that the establishment set out in the chart on page 7 be adopted by schwere Panzer-Abteilungen 502 and 503, which were in the process of formation, and on 21 October 1942 this was extended to schwere Panzer-Abteilung 501. Each battalion was made up of twenty Tigers and twenty-five Pzkpfw III light tanks and initially the latter were armed with the 5cm gun but numbers of Pzkpfw III ausf N tanks, equipped with a 7.5cm weapon, were allocated as they became available. The battalion contained a Stabskompanie, or headquarters company, with two Tigers and one Pzkpfw III. The headquarters company also controlled a platoon of five Pzkpfw III tanks as well as anti-aircraft and maintenance units. The battalion's two tank companies were each controlled by a headquarters troop of a single Tiger and two Pzkpfw III tanks and were made up of four platoons of two Tigers and two Pzkpfw IIIs. This was of course the ideal and, as we shall see, rarely achieved in the period covered by this study.

With minor differences for schwere Panzer-Abteilungen 504 and 505, this structure remained in place until 5 March 1943 when a complete reorganisation saw the light tanks removed and the companies reduced to three platoons of four Tigers each. The number of companies in a battalion was, however, increased to three meaning that a complete schwere Panzer-Abteilung could now field forty-five tanks.

In November 1942, in addition to the heavy Panzer battalions, Tiger companies were formed for the three SS-Panzer-Regiments which had been formed up to that time and in January 1943 a Tiger company was raised for Panzer-Regiment Grossdeutschland.

Following are brief histories of the heavy Panzer units which served on the Eastern Front from August 1942, when the first tanks arrived, until the end of March 1943.

A January production Tiger I of 13.Kompanie, Panzer-Regiment Grossdeutschland. The turret number, S20, indicates the commander of the company's 2.Zug. Note the oversized stowage box which was a feature of many of this company's Tigers. Note also the Balkenkreuz national insignia on the hull rear plate next to the muffler cover.

This initial production Tiger I, assembled in August 1942, was one of the four tanks of 1.Kompanie, schwere Panzer-Abteilung 502 that were sent to the Eastern Front to take part in the battles south of Leningrad. None were fitted with stowage boxes and the example seen here was fabricated in the field. The company number 100 is just visible on the side. Note the extensions fitted to the exhaust mufflers which were a common feature of these tanks. This vehicle is also shown and discussed on page 17 of the Camouflage & Markings section of this book.

Schwere Panzer-Abteilung 502. Formed on 25 May 1942 from Panzer-Ersatz-Abteilung 35, this unit was not the first of the heavy tank battalions created by the German Army, as is sometimes stated, although it was the first to receive an allocation of Tigers and the first to see action.

The first two tanks were delivered on Wednesday, 19 August 1942 and a further two arrived on the next day. But by the following Sunday these four vehicles were being loaded onto railway cars and sent via Hanover and Schneidemühl to the Eastern Front.

The Tigers, referred to as 1.Kompanie, were accompanied by the battalion commander, Major Richard Märker, with his headquarters staff and about half the battalion's maintenance company (1). Hitler had personally ordered that the Tigers be employed in the battles around Leningrad, modern-day St Petersburg, in the hope of ending the siege of the city and the stalemate that had existed on the northern edge of the front since late 1941.

On 29 August 1942 the tanks were unloaded at Mga, south-east of Leningrad, and immediately ordered to move towards the front and take up defensive positions. Reluctantly, Major Märker ordered his men forward but three of the Tigers broke down due to transmission problems and the fourth withdrew before any contact was made with the enemy. Although unsettling, this could hardly have been unexpected as these first models suffered almost continuous mechanical failures and during the training phase were only kept operational with the help of civilian maintenance crews from the Henschel factory temporarily attached to the battalion.

On 16 September 1942 two new Tigers were delivered, bringing the battalion's total to six, and these were all initial production models assembled in August. Two days later a further Tiger was delivered and this vehicle must have been one of the first of the September production run. On 21 September 1942 the battalion at last went into action in a series of limited attacks near Tortolovo, about 10 kilometres east of Mga, in support of 170.Infanterie-Division. Interestingly, just four of the available seven Tigers took part in this operation suggesting that the remainder were in repair.

During the assault one Tiger was disabled by enemy fire and three were bogged down in the swampy terrain and although three of these vehicles were later recovered, one tank was so close to the Russian lines that it could not be reached and was under constant enemy fire. Repeated requests by Major Märker that this tank be destroyed were denied. On 30 September the battalion was withdrawn to Tossno, 20 kilometres to the south-west, and reported that nine Tigers, the full complement for a single company, and twenty-five Pzkpfw III tanks were on hand (2).

Notes

1. In addition to the Tigers there may have been as many as nine Pzkpfw III ausf L tanks but I have been unable to confirm this.
2. This number was made up of eighteen Pzkpfw III ausf L and seven Pzkpfw III ausf N, the authorised total for a complete battalion.

............text continued on page 11

SCHWERE PANZER-ABTEILUNG 502, DECEMBER 1942

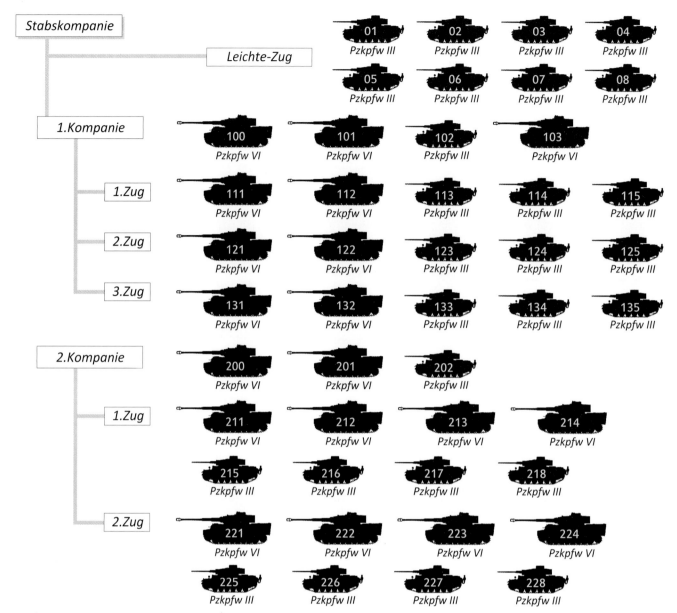

EQUIPMENT ALLOCATIONS AND LOSSES, SCHWERE PANZER-ABTEILUNG 502

Tiger I. 1.Kp	Aug 1942	Sep 1942	Oct 1942	Nov 1942	Dec 1942	Jan 1943	Feb 1943	Mar 1943
Received	6	2 (2)	2 (4)	0	0	0	7	0
Lost	0	0	0	1 (5)	0	5 (6)	1	2
On hand	6	8	9	8	8	3	9	7
Operational	4 (1)	7 (3)			7	1	4	4
Tiger I. 2.Kp	Aug 1942	Sep 1942	Oct 1942	Nov 1942	Dec 1942	Jan 1943	Feb 1943	Mar 1943
Received		2	0	0	9	0		
Lost		0	2 (7)	0	0	0		
On hand		2	0	0	9	9 (8)		
Operational		2	0	0	9	9		

1. The four serviceable tanks, all initial production models, were the only Tigers to be sent Russia at this time. 2. Received on 16 and 18 September 1942. That is, after the initial four Tigers had left for the Eastern Front. 3. One Tiger was bogged down during the attack on Tortolovo, south of Leningrad, and although it was essentially in running order it was under constant enemy fire and could not be recovered. Permission to destroy it in place was denied at the highest level. 4. These tanks were transferred from 2.Kompanie which was still training in Germany. 5. Permission was finally given to destroy the tank abandoned near Tortolovo. 6. One of these tanks was Tiger 100 which is discussed elsewhere in this book and depicted on page 17 of the Camouflage & Markings section. 7. These are the two Tigers transferred to 1.Kompanie. 8. Towards the end of the month 2.Kompanie was permanently attached to schwere Panzer-Abteilung 503 as the battalion's third company. A new 2.Kompanie for schwere Panzer-Abteilung 502 was not formed until April 1943.

............text continued from page 9

Blamed for the poor performance of his unit, Major Märker was relieved of his command on 21 November 1942 and replaced by Hauptmann Artur Wollschläger. A few days later permission was finally granted to destroy the Tiger abandoned in the woods near Tortolovo in September.

The battalion's 2.Kompanie was formed from surplus crews of Panzer-Regiment 1 and Panzer-Regiment 35 and arrived in Russia on 7 January 1943 to be attached to Heeresgruppe Don operating in the southern Ukraine, far from 1.Kompanie which was fighting on the Volkov. But it seems the lessons of 1942 had been learnt as the company's nine Tigers were able to complete the road march from Proletarsk, south-east of Rostov, crossing the Kuberle River towards modern-day Gashun, a journey of over 100 kilometres, on their own tracks without a single mechanical failure. It is likely that these tanks were all assembled in December.

On 22 February 1943 the battalion's second company was transferred to schwere Panzer-Abteilung 503 and renamed as that formation's third company. While 1.Kompanie remained in the Leningrad area, a new 2.Kompanie was formed in France from men of Panzer-Regiment 3 by the end of April 1943.

Schwere Panzer-Abteilung 503. Formed with two companies on 16 April 1942 from tank crews of Panzer-Regiment 5 and Panzer-Regiment 6, this battalion had trained briefly on the Porsche Tiger before the decision was made to manufacture the Henschel version. Originally intended for service in North Africa, the first Tigers were received in November 1942. In his three-volume study of the Tiger battalions Oberst Wolfgang Schneider states that the battalion's tanks were 'modified for hot-climate employment' on 19 November but does not clarify what this entailed. Given that just four tanks were on hand at this time it may have meant that they were fitted with the Feifel air-filtering system or that they were simply painted in the authorised North African camouflage colours (1).

A further sixteen Tigers were received in December 1942, all assembled in the same month, bringing the battalion's total to twenty Tigers and thirty-one Pzkpfw III ausf N tanks. Schneider mentions that on 16 December all vehicles were modified 'for employment on the Eastern Front'. Again, there is no detailed explanation of what this may mean but many photographs of the battalion's Tigers show that they are not equipped with the Feifel air-filters although the V-shaped duct for the hoses can be seen, suggesting that at some time the filters were attached.

The battalion was sent to the Eastern Front in January 1943 and took part in the defensive battles following the retreat from the Caucasus. On 22 January the second company of schwere Panzer-Abteilung 502, which had been attached and operating under the battalion's command for some time, was formally transferred and became 3.Kompanie, schwere Panzer-Abteilung 503.

............text continued on page 13

Notes

1. Feifel air-filters were introduced into production in November although the brackets to hold them had been standard fittings since the previous month. As discussed in the Technical Details and Modifications section, the first four Tigers allocated to this battalion may have been assembled in the first half of November.

The Tigers of 2.Kompanie, schwere Panzer-Abteilung 502 arrived on the Eastern Front in January 1943 but did not join the battalion in the Leningrad area. Instead they were diverted to southern Ukraine and subordinated to Heeresgruppe Don. The battalion's charging mammoth unit insignia is just visible on the right-hand corner of the hull front. This tank, number 211, was renumbered as 300 when the company was officially absorbed by schwere Panzer-Abteilung 503.

SCHWERE PANZER-ABTEILUNG 503, DECEMEBER 1942

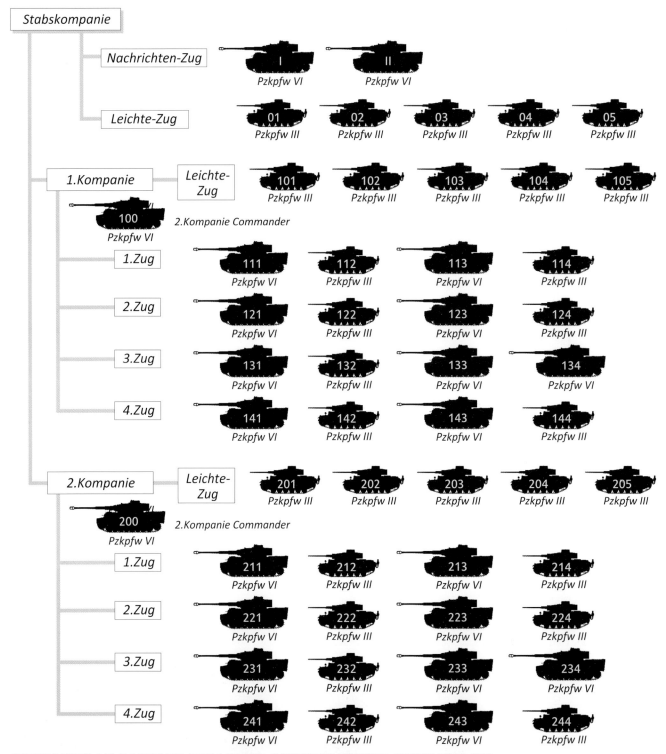

EQUIPMENT ALLOCATIONS AND LOSSES, SCHWERE PANZER-ABTEILUNG 503

Tiger I.	Aug 1942	Sep 1942	Oct 1942	Nov 1942	Dec 1942	Jan 1943	Feb 1943	Mar 1943
Received				4	16	9 (1)	0	10
Lost				0	0	5 (2)	1	2 (3)
On hand				4	20	24	23	31
Operational				4	20	7	2	19 (4)

1. These nine tanks are the Tigers of 2.Kompanie, schwere Panzer-Abteilung 502 which were transferred to the battalion on 22 January 1943. There is some argument about the exact date and this figure is sometimes included in the March numbers for this battalion and also, less helpfully, in both months, giving a completely incorrect on-hand figure. 2. Two of these tanks were lost to enemy action, one was destroyed by its own crew and two more were damaged so comprehensively that they were sent back to Germany. One of the latter, Tiger 231, is shown on page 24 of the Camouflage & Markings section. 3. Both tanks were returned to Germany for long-term repair. 4. I am assuming here that the ten new tanks, which arrived on the last day of the month, were all operational.

...........text continued from page 11

Panzer-Regiment-Grossdeutschland. As a fully-motorised infantry formation the Grossdeutschland (GD) division had received a tank battalion in early 1942 comprising a staff and three medium tank companies. In January 1943 the battalion was upgraded to a full regiment with a second battalion formed from II.Abteilung, Panzer-Regiment 203. The original tank battalion was renamed I.Abteilung, Panzer-Regiment GD on 3 March 1943 when the second battalion reached the front.

Also attached to the second battalion was the newly-raised heavy company. Created on 5 February 1943 from 3.Kompanie, Panzer-Regiment 203 and named 13.Kompanie, Panzer-Regiment GD (1), the company arrived in Russia in late February with just nine Tigers. These were all January 1943 production versions with the escape hatch fitted to the turret side on the right in place of the pistol port. Many, but not all, had large stowage boxes that were probably fabricated by the battalion's workshops and these are examined in the Technical Details and Modifications section. The company did not receive any replacements until May 1943.

As part of Kampfgruppe Strachwitz the company took part in the fighting around Kharkov, particularly near modern-day Koviahy, where twenty Russian tanks were destroyed in a single action. By mid-March the company was reduced to a single serviceable Tiger and towards the end of the month the remaining vehicles were withdrawn to Poltava to rest and refit.

Notes

1. Sources differ on this date with Jentz giving 13 February 1943 while Schneider suggests the date shown here. Almost all agree that the first tanks were not allocated before February 1943.

13.KOMPANIE, PANZER-REGIMENT GROSSDEUTSCHLAND, FEBRUARY 1943

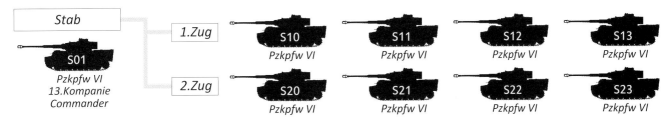

Stab

S01
Pzkpfw VI
13.Kompanie
Commander

1.Zug — S10 Pzkpfw VI | S11 Pzkpfw VI | S12 Pzkpfw VI | S13 Pzkpfw VI

2.Zug — S20 Pzkpfw VI | S21 Pzkpfw VI | S22 Pzkpfw VI | S23 Pzkpfw VI

EQUIPMENT ALLOCATIONS AND LOSSES, 13.KOMPANIE, PANZER-REGIMENT GD

Tiger I.	Aug 1942	Sep 1942	Oct 1942	Nov 1942	Dec 1942	Jan 1943	Feb 1943	Mar 1943
Received						7	2	0
Lost						0	0	0
On hand						7	9	9
Operational						7	4	1 (1)

1. Numbers given for operational tanks can be quite misleading and it should be remembered that unless a vehicle was severely damaged it would be retained by the battalion or division repair units and returned to service at some later time, often within days. The nine original tanks allocated to this company were all under repair at all some time but were back with their crews by the end of April 1943.

This Befehlspanzerwagen command tank is based on an early production Tiger assembled in January 1943. The first tanks allocated to this company were painted in RAL Gebbraun 8000 with a disruptive pattern of Graugrun RAL 7008, the first North African camouflage, after assembly and the contrast with the black of the Balkenkreuz is obvious here. Note that the latter is partly covered by the trackguards.

Notes

1. The three Waffen-SS divisions mentioned here were all classed as Panzergrenadier divisions until late 1943 when all were upgraded to Panzer divisions.

SS-Panzer-Regiment 1. Formed in late November 1942 as 4.Kompanie, SS-Panzer-Regiment 1, with personnel drawn from the regiment's own establishment, the new heavy company received ten Tigers and fifteen Pzkpfw III ausf J tanks on 21 January 1943. The Tigers were all manufactured in December 1942 and as a field modification many tanks had spare track links fitted to the hull front.

The company took part in the offensive to recapture Kharkov in February and March 1943 together with the Tigers of the Das Reich and Totenkopf divisions (1). In mid-March the Tigers of 4.Kompanie, as part of Kampfgruppe Peiper, were diverted to Belgorod, 40 kilometres north-east of Kharkov, in an attempt to cut off retreating Soviet units.

This operation resulted in a stalemate after a fierce firefight near Gonki on the Belgorod to Kursk road and the remaining Tigers were withdrawn to Kharkov, which was now firmly in German hands.

4.KOMPANIE, SS-PANZER-REGIMENT 1, FEBRUARY 1943

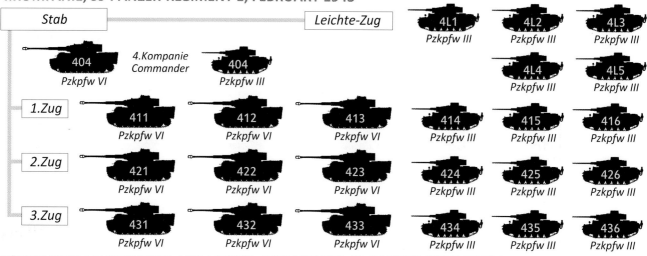

EQUIPMENT ALLOCATIONS AND LOSSES, 4.KOMPANIE, SS-PANZER-REGIMENT 1

Tiger I.	Aug 1942	Sep 1942	Oct 1942	Nov 1942	Dec 1942	Jan 1943	Feb 1943	Mar 1943
Received					6	4	0	0
Lost					0	0	1 (1)	1 (2)
On hand					6	10	9	8
Operational					6	10	8	5

1. After being damaged beyond repair by an internal fire, this Tiger was destroyed by its own crew. 2. For reasons I cannot explain, this tank, another victim of an internal fire, is often included in the February losses although the company's records are quite clear. Commanded by Unterscharführer Jürgen Brandt, it was destroyed by its own crew somewhere west of the Kharkov to Krasnograd road, probably between the present-day villages of Bilukhivka and Mykolo-Komyshuvta.

An early production Tiger I of 2.Zug, 4.Kompanie, SS-Panzer-Regiment 1 photographed during the battles to retake Kharkov. Like many tanks of this company this Tiger has an oversized stowage box held in place by a single metal bracket at the top. The Feifel air-filters are in place but the hoses seem to be missing. Note the style of Balkenkreuz, which seems to have been common to the Tigers allocated to the Waffen-SS regiments in late 1942, and the high contrast between the black of the cross an the base colour of the tank, which is probably Braun RAL 8020.

SS-Panzer-Regiment 2. Created at the same time as the heavy company of SS-Panzer-Regiment 1, this unit's formation began in early December 1942 at Fallingbostel while a number of crews were trained at the Henschel works in Kassel. In the same month the company received its first Tigers and all were December 1942 models. At some time before the unit left for the front in late January 1943 it was named 8.Kompanie, SS-Panzer-Regiment 2. In March, as part of Kampfgruppe Das Reich, the company took part in the recapture of Kharkov and the fighting to the north-east of the city. By the end of the month none of the Tigers were considered operational although eight were in short-term repair and seven of the Pzkpfw III vehicles still took part in the fighting.

8.KOMPANIE, SS-PANZER-REGIMENT 2, FEBRUARY 1943

EQUIPMENT ALLOCATIONS AND LOSSES, 8.KOMPANIE, SS-PANZER-REGIMENT 2

Tiger I.	Aug 1942	Sep 1942	Oct 1942	Nov 1942	Dec 1942	Jan 1943	Feb 1943	Mar 1943
Received					2	8	1 (1)	0
Lost						0	1 (2)	2 (3)
On hand					2	10	10	8
Operational					2	10	3	4

1. This Tiger was a Befehlspanzerwagen command tank. 2. This tank was abandoned by its crew after being disabled and was later captured, largely intact, by the Russians. 3. One tank was lost to enemy action and during an attack near Merefa, a small town on the Kharkov to Poltava railway line, on the first day of the month, another tank caught fire and was completely burnt out.

Photographed in Kharkov in March 1943 this tank, Tiger 832 of 8.Kompanie, SS-Panzer-Regiment 2, was built in January 1943 and allocated to the company in the same month. Note that the whitewash camouflage has been largely worn away from the turret stowage box revealing what is probably a base coat of Braun RAL 8020. This vehicle, Fgst Nr.250085, is also depicted on page 26 of the Camouflage & Markings section.

Notes

1. This unit's history is covered in some detail in *TankCraft 20, Tiger I: German Heavy Tank Eastern Front, Summer 1943*.

SS-Panzer-Regiment 3. Formed as 9.Kompanie, SS-Panzer-Regiment 3 at the same time as the heavy companies of the other Waffen-SS divisions.

The tank crews were drafted from replacement personnel of SS-Panzer-Regiment 1 and SS-Panzer-Regiment 2 with some men from the reconnaissance platoons and the first and second battalions of SS-Panzer-Regiment 3. The first Tigers were received during January 1943 and were all models assembled in that month. By 10 February the company was ordered to the Russian Front. The company went into action for the first time on 21 February 1943 near Pavlograd on the Samara river in eastern Ukraine, attacking through an intense snowstorm. The Tigers of 9.Kompanie supported operations by the Adolf Hitler and Das Reich divisions until 17 March when they were reunited with SS-Panzer-Regiment 3 at which time just three tanks were in a serviceable condition (1).

4.KOMPANIE, SS-PANZER-REGIMENT 3, JANUARY 1943

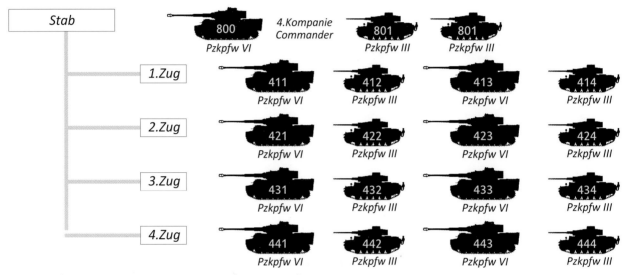

Stab			

800 — 4.Kompanie Commander — Pzkpfw VI
801 — Pzkpfw III
801 — Pzkpfw III

1.Zug
411 — Pzkpfw VI
412 — Pzkpfw III
413 — Pzkpfw VI
414 — Pzkpfw III

2.Zug
421 — Pzkpfw VI
422 — Pzkpfw III
423 — Pzkpfw VI
424 — Pzkpfw III

3.Zug
431 — Pzkpfw VI
432 — Pzkpfw III
433 — Pzkpfw VI
434 — Pzkpfw III

4.Zug
441 — Pzkpfw VI
442 — Pzkpfw III
443 — Pzkpfw VI
444 — Pzkpfw III

EQUIPMENT ALLOCATIONS AND LOSSES, 4.KOMPANIE, SS-PANZER-REGIMENT 3

Tiger I.	Aug 1942	Sep 1942	Oct 1942	Nov 1942	Dec 1942	Jan 1943	Feb 1943	Mar 1943
Received						9	0	0
Lost						0	1 (1)	2 (2)
On hand						9	8	6
Operational						9	6	2

1. This Tiger was completely submerged after breaking through an ice-covered river near modern-day Pereschepyne on the Dnipro to Kharkov road. It was consigned to a rear-area repair depot and it is not clear if it was returned to the company. 2. One of these tanks was another victim of breaking ice and could not be recovered until April. The other was lost due to the premature ignition of an 8.8cm shell which also killed the company commander, Hauptsturmführer Alois Mooslechner.

At left: Tiger I and Pzkpfw III ausf L tanks of 1.Zug, 4.Kompanie, SS-Panzer-Regiment 3 possibly photographed north of Krasnograd where the regiment assembled for the assault on Kharkov in early March 1943. Note the relatively neat and uniform application of whitewash and the turret numbers.

At right: Tiger 821 of 8.Kompanie, SS-Panzer-Regiment 2 pictured just prior to the attack on Olschany near Belrorod on 10 March 1943. The tank's commander, Obersturmführer Phillip Theiss, is standing in the foreground wearing a fur cap. Note the small Mickey Mouse logo on the hull front. This does not seem to have been retained when the tank was repainted and renumbered as 813 in the spring.

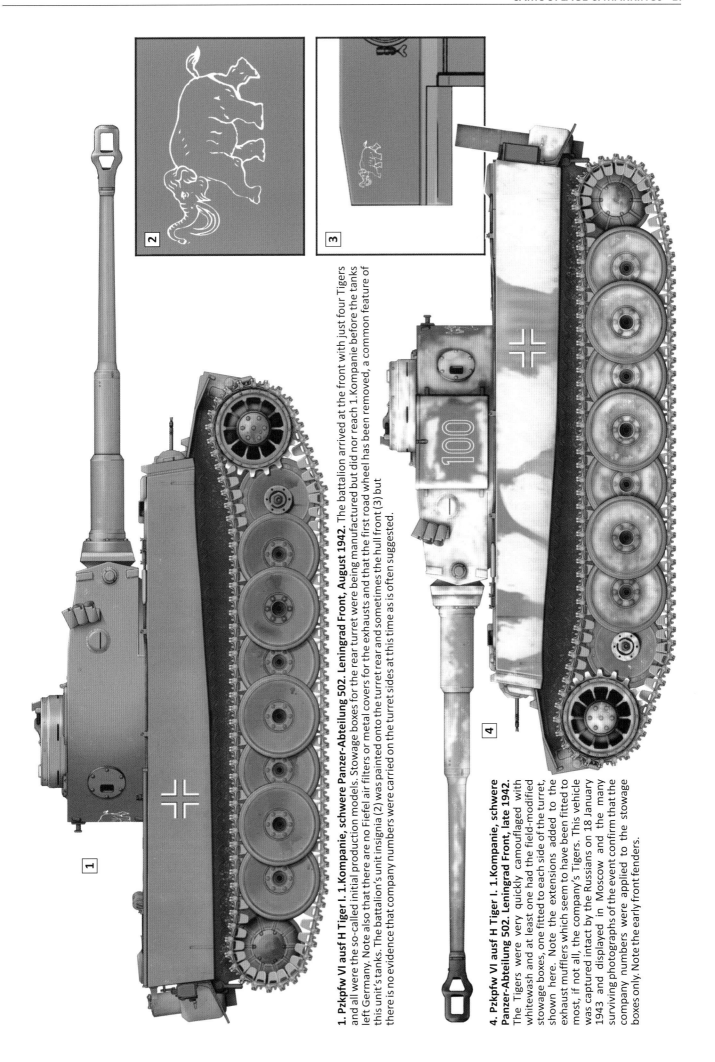

1. Pzkpfw VI ausf H Tiger I. 1.Kompanie, schwere Panzer-Abteilung 502. Leningrad Front, August 1942. The battalion arrived at the front with just four Tigers and all were the so-called initial production models. Stowage boxes for the rear turret were being manufactured but did nor reach 1.Kompanie before the tanks left Germany. Note also that there are no Fiefel air filters or metal covers for the exhausts and that the first road wheel has been removed, a common feature of this unit's tanks. The battalion's unit insignia (2) was painted onto the turret rear and sometimes the hull front (3) but there is no evidence that company numbers were carried on the turret sides at this time as is often suggested.

4. Pzkpfw VI ausf H Tiger I. 1.Kompanie, schwere Panzer-Abteilung 502. Leningrad Front, late 1942. The Tigers were very quickly camouflaged with whitewash and at least one had the field-modified stowage boxes, one fitted to each side of the turret, shown here. Note the extensions added to the exhaust mufflers which seem to have been fitted to most, if not all, the company's Tigers. This vehicle was captured intact by the Russians on 18 January 1943 and displayed in Moscow and the many surviving photographs of the event confirm that the company numbers were applied to the stowage boxes only. Note the early front fenders.

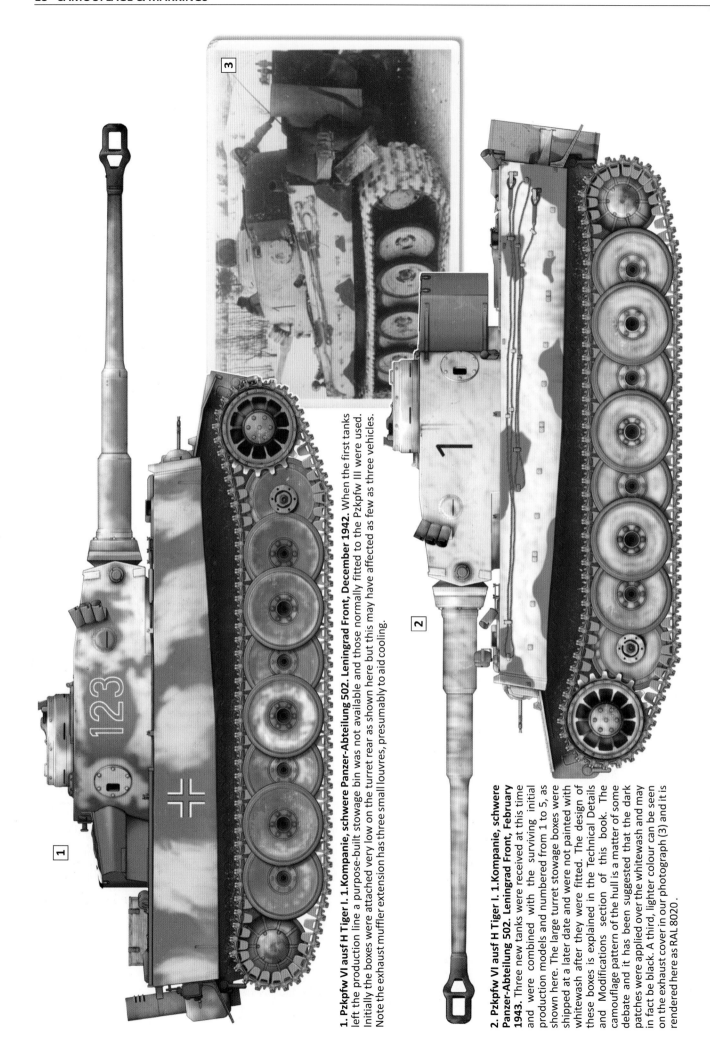

1. Pzkpfw VI ausf H Tiger I. 1.Kompanie, schwere Panzer-Abteilung 502. Leningrad Front, December 1942. When the first tanks left the production line a purpose-built stowage bin was not available and those normally fitted to the Pzkpfw III were used. Initially the boxes were attached very low on the turret rear as shown here but this may have affected as few as three vehicles. Note the exhaust muffler extension has three small louvres, presumably to aid cooling.

2. Pzkpfw VI ausf H Tiger I. 1.Kompanie, schwere Panzer-Abteilung 502. Leningrad Front, February 1943. Three new tanks were received at this time and were combined with the surviving initial production models and numbered from 1 to 5, as shown here. The large turret stowage boxes were shipped at a later date and were not painted with whitewash after they were fitted. The design of these boxes is explained in the Technical Details and Modifications section of this book. The camouflage pattern of the hull is a matter of some debate and it has been suggested that the dark patches were applied over the whitewash and may in fact be black. A third, lighter colour can be seen on the exhaust cover in our photograph (3) and it is rendered here as RAL 8020.

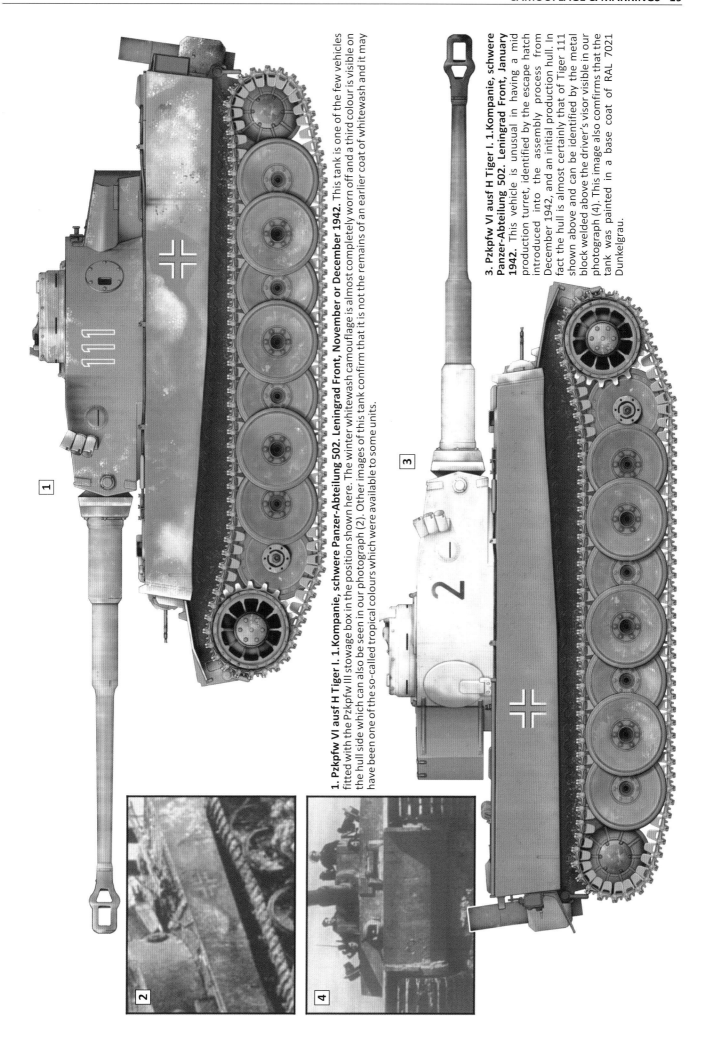

1. Pzkpfw VI ausf H Tiger I. 1.Kompanie, schwere Panzer-Abteilung 502. Leningrad Front, November or December 1942. This tank is one of the few vehicles fitted with the Pzkpfw III stowage box in the position shown here. The winter whitewash camouflage is almost completely worn off and a third colour is visible on the hull side which can also be seen in our photograph (2). Other images of this tank confirm that it is not the remains of an earlier coat of whitewash and it may have been one of the so-called tropical colours which were available to some units.

3. Pzkpfw VI ausf H Tiger I. 1.Kompanie, schwere Panzer-Abteilung 502. Leningrad Front, January 1942. This vehicle is unusual in having a mid production turret, identified by the escape hatch introduced into the assembly process from December 1942, and an initial production hull. In fact the hull is almost certainly that of Tiger 111 shown above and can be identified by the metal block welded above the driver's visor visible in our photograph (4). This image also comfirms that the tank was painted in a base coat of RAL 7021 Dunkelgrau.

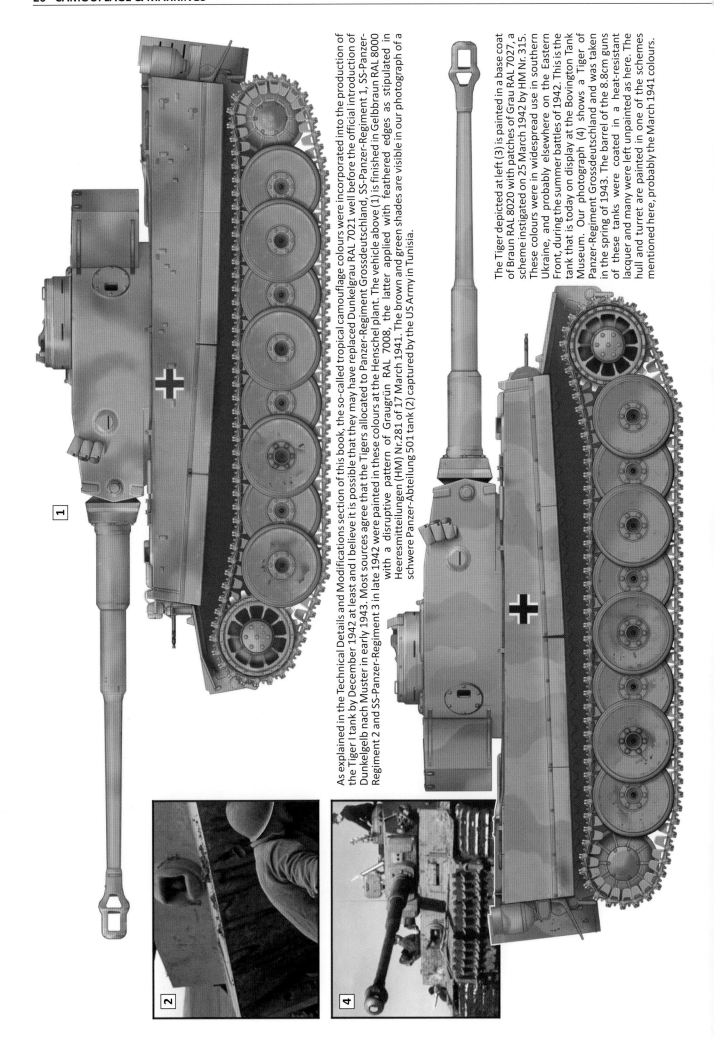

As explained in the Technical Details and Modifications section of this book, the so-called tropical camouflage colours were incorporated into the production of the Tiger I tank by December 1942 at least and I believe it is possible that they may have replaced Dunkelgrau RAL 7021 well before the official introduction of Dunkelgelb nach Muster in early 1943. Most sources agree that the Tigers allocated to Panzer-Regiment Grossdeutschland, SS-Panzer-Regiment 1, SS-Panzer-Regiment 2 and SS-Panzer-Regiment 3 in late 1942 were painted in these colours at the Henschel plant. The vehicle above (1) is finished in Gelbbraun RAL 8000 with a disruptive pattern of Graugrün RAL 7008, the latter applied with feathered edges as stipulated in Heeresmitteilungen (HM) Nr.281 of 17 March 1941. The brown and green shades are visible in our photograph of a schwere Panzer-Abteilung 501 tank (2) captured by the US Army in Tunisia.

The Tiger depicted at left (3) is painted in a base coat of Braun RAL 8020 with patches of Grau RAL 7027, a scheme instigated on 25 March 1942 by HM Nr. 315. These colours were in widespread use in southern Ukraine, and probably elsewhere on the Eastern Front, during the summer battles of 1942. This is the tank that is today on display at the Bovington Tank Museum. Our photograph (4) shows a Tiger of Panzer-Regiment Grossdeutschland and was taken in the spring of 1943. The barrel of the 8.8cm guns of these tanks were coated in a heat-resistant lacquer and many were left unpainted as here. The hull and turret are painted in one of the schemes mentioned here, probably the March 1941 colours.

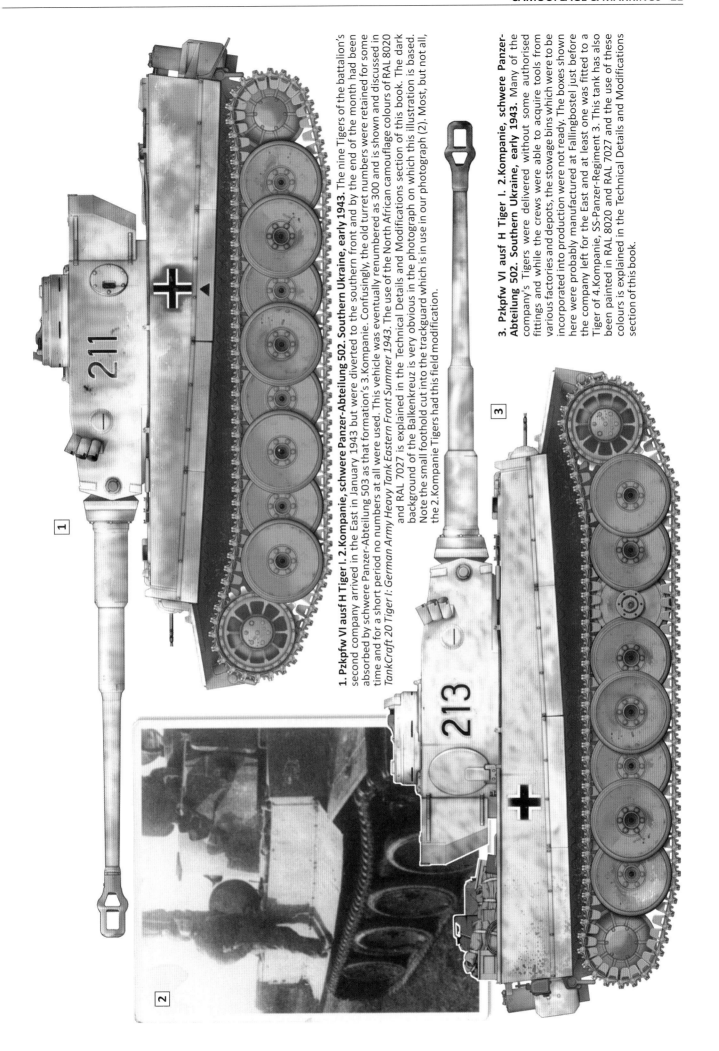

1. Pzkpfw VI ausf H Tiger I. 2.Kompanie, schwere Panzer-Abteilung 502. Southern Ukraine, early 1943. The nine Tigers of the battalion's second company arrived in the East in January 1943 but were diverted to the southern front and by the end of the month had been absorbed by schwere Panzer-Abteilung 503 as that formation's 3.Kompanie. Confusingly, the old turret numbers were retained for some time and for a short period no numbers at all were used. This vehicle was eventually renumbered as 300 and is shown and discussed in *TankCraft 20 Tiger I: German Army Heavy Tank Eastern Front Summer 1943*. The use of the North African camouflage colours of RAL 8020 and RAL 7027 is explained in the Technical Details and Modifications section of this book. The dark background of the Balkenkreuz is very obvious in the photograph on which this illustration is based. Note the small foothold cut into the trackguard which is in use in our photograph (2). Most, but not all, the 2.Kompanie Tigers had this field modification.

3. Pzkpfw VI ausf H Tiger I. 2.Kompanie, schwere Panzer-Abteilung 502. Southern Ukraine, early 1943. Many of the company's Tigers were delivered without some authorised fittings and while the crews were able to acquire tools from various factories and depots, the stowage bins which were to be incorporated into production were not ready. The boxes shown here were probably manufactured at Fallingbostel just before the company left for the East and at least one was fitted to a Tiger of 4.Kompanie, SS-Panzer-Regiment 3. This tank has also been painted in RAL 8020 and RAL 7027 and the use of these colours is explained in the Technical Details and Modifications section of this book.

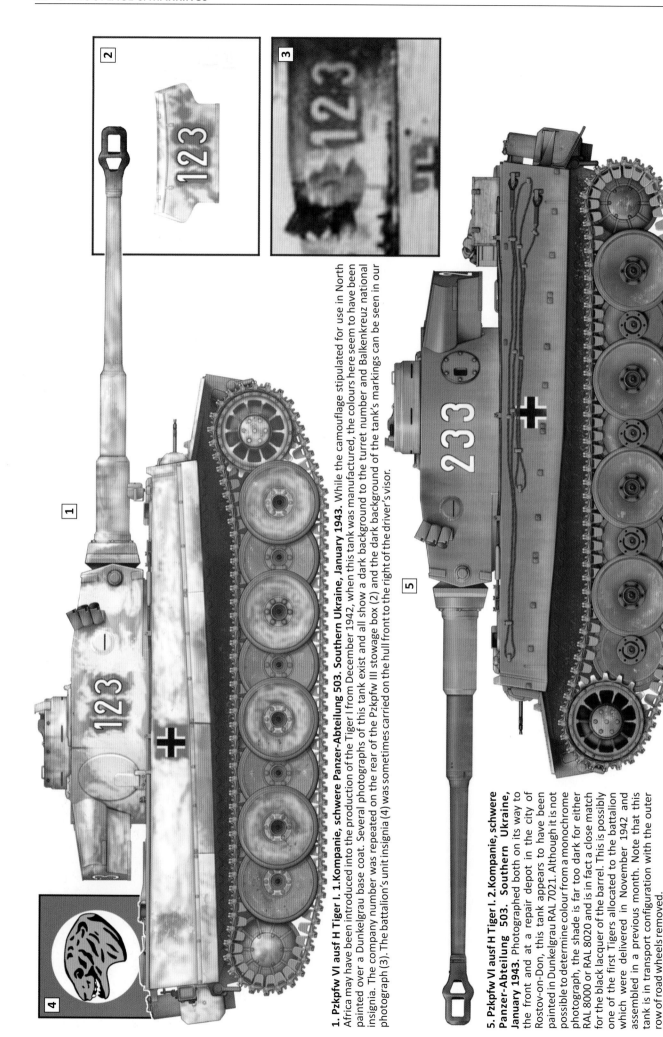

1. Pzkpfw VI ausf H Tiger I. 1.Kompanie, schwere Panzer-Abteilung 503. Southern Ukraine, January 1943. While the camouflage stipulated for use in North Africa may have been introduced into the production of the Tiger I from December 1942, when this tank was manufactured, the colours here seem to have been painted over a Dunkelgrau base coat. Several photographs of this tank exist and all show a dark background to the turret number and Balkenkreuz national insignia. The company number was repeated on the rear of the Pzkpfw III stowage box (2) and the dark background of the tank's markings can be seen in our photograph (3). The battalion's unit insignia (4) was sometimes carried on the hull front to the right of the driver's visor.

5. Pzkpfw VI ausf H Tiger I. 2.Kompanie, schwere Panzer-Abteilung 503. Southern Ukraine, January 1943. Photographed both on its way to the front and at a repair depot in the city of Rostov-on-Don, this tank appears to have been painted in Dunkelgrau RAL 7021. Although it is not possible to determine colour from a monochrome photograph, the shade is far too dark for either RAL 8000 or RAL 8020 and is in fact a close match for the black lacquer of the barrel. This is possibly one of the first Tigers allocated to the battalion which were delivered in November 1942 and assembled in a previous month. Note that this tank is in transport configuration with the outer row of road wheels removed.

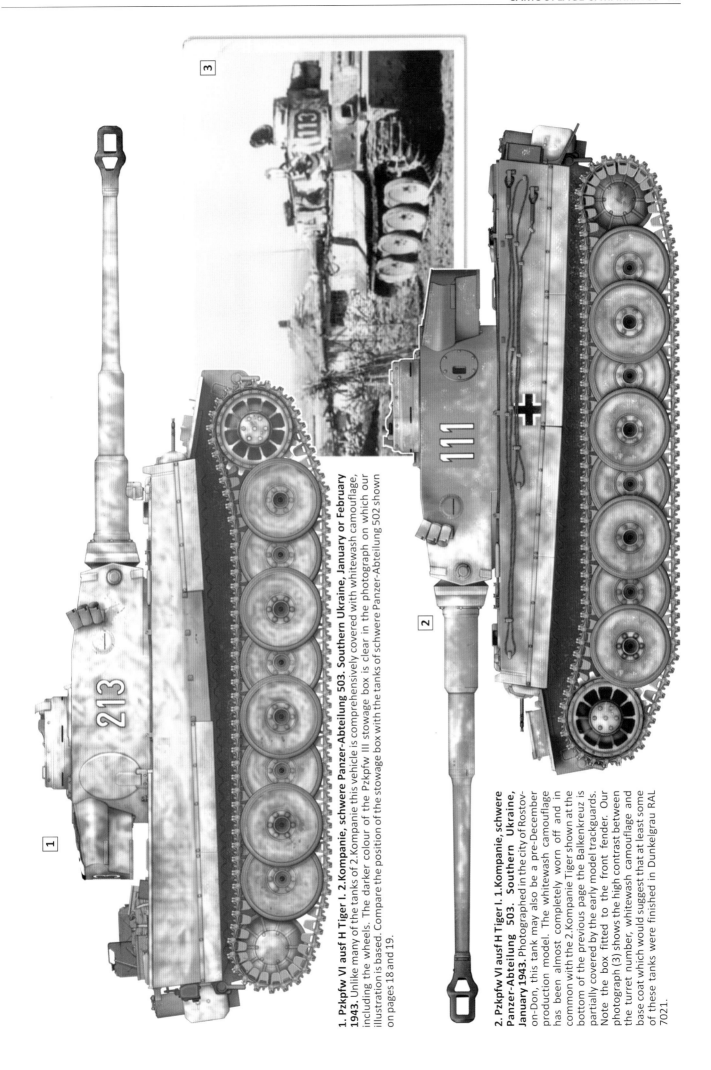

1. Pzkpfw VI ausf H Tiger I. 2.Kompanie, schwere Panzer-Abteilung 503. Southern Ukraine, January or February 1943. Unlike many of the tanks of 2.Kompanie this vehicle is comprehensively covered with whitewash camouflage, including the wheels. The darker colour of the Pzkpfw III stowage box is clear in the photograph on which our illustration is based. Compare the position of the stowage box with tanks of schwere Panzer-Abteilung 502 shown on pages 18 and 19.

2. Pzkpfw VI ausf H Tiger I. 1.Kompanie, schwere Panzer-Abteilung 503. Southern Ukraine, January 1943. Photographed in the city of Rostov-on-Don, this tank may also be a pre-December production model. The whitewash camouflage has been almost completely worn off and in common with the 2.Kompanie Tiger shown at the bottom of the previous page the Balkenkreuz is partially covered by the early model trackguards. Note the box fitted to the front fender. Our photograph (3) shows the high contrast between the turret number, whitewash camouflage and base coat which would suggest that at least some of these tanks were finished in Dunkelgrau RAL 7021.

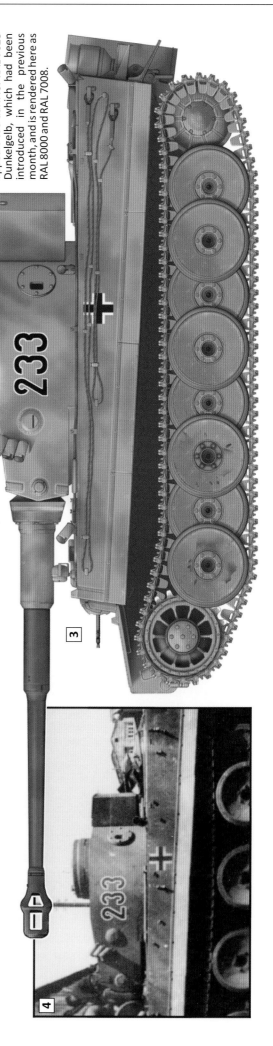

1. Pzkpfw VI ausf H Tiger I. 2.Kompanie, schwere Panzer-Abteilung 503. Southern Ukraine, January 1943. Commanded by Leutnant Friedrich Zabel, this tank was involved in the fighting along the Manych River where in a single action it survived over 250 hits by Russian tank and anti-tank guns. It was returned to Germany but could not be completely repaired and the turret was used at Paderborn to train loaders and gunners. The vehicle became famous after it was featured in the *Tigerfibel*, a training manual issued to Tiger crews (2). This tank almost certainly left the production line in a camouflage scheme of RAL 8020 and RAL 7027. The Dunkelgrau stowage box is speculation on my part.

3. Pzkpfw VI ausf H Tiger I. 2.Kompanie, schwere Panzer-Abteilung 503. Kharkov area, spring 1943. In late March the battalion received ten new tanks and this February production model may be one of those. Initially allocated to 1.Kompanie, they were all later split between 2.Kompanie and 3.Kompanie and at this time the black turret numbers shown here were adopted.

The camouflage pattern evident in our photograph (4) appears too dark for RAL 7028 Dunkelgelb, which had been introduced in the previous month, and is rendered here as RAL 8000 and RAL 7008.

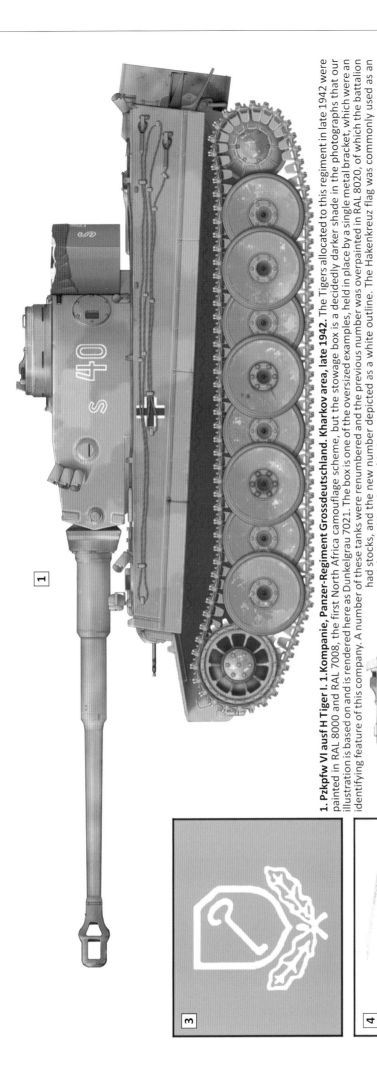

1. Pzkpfw VI ausf H Tiger I. 1.Kompanie, Panzer-Regiment Grossdeutschland. Kharkov area, late 1942. The Tigers allocated to this regiment in late 1942 were painted in RAL 8000 and RAL 7008, the first North Africa camouflage scheme, but the stowage box is a decidedly darker shade in the photographs that our illustration is based on and is rendered here as Dunkelgrau 7021. The box is one of the oversized examples, held in place by a single metal bracket, which were an identifying feature of this company. A number of these tanks were renumbered and the previous number was overpainted in RAL 8020, of which the battalion had stocks, and the new number depicted as a white outline. The Hakenkreuz flag was commonly used as an aerial recognition sign at this time.

2. Pzkpfw VI ausf H Tiger I. 4.Kompanie, SS-Panzer-Regiment 1. Kharkov area, early 1942. The company arrived in the East during the first two weeks of February with ten Tigers and all were post-December production models with the turret escape hatch as depicted here. Not shown are the spare track links which most tanks carried on the hull front. The tanks left the factory in the North African colours of RAL 8020 and RAL 7027 and all were painted in whitewash camouflage, with the company number neatly avoided as seen here, before going into action. Note that part of the Fiefel air filter is missing. This vehicle was repainted and renumbered as 1311 in April 1943 and later took part in the fighting around Prokhorovka during Operation Citadel. The regiment's unit insignia (3) was carried by most tanks in the position shown here (4).

1. Pzkpfw VI ausf H Tiger I. 4.Kompanie, SS-Panzer-Regiment 3. Southern Ukraine, early 1943. The company's nine Tigers were all numbered in the 400 series, as shown here, and the numbers were depicted in a very dark colour, probably black. All the Tigers were fitted with Feifel air filters, sheet metal covers for the exhaust mufflers, turret escape hatch and straight-edged trackguards. Note that part of the cupola has been removed, almost certainly due to battle damage, and the upper ring and hatch has been fitted into the resulting aperture. Later photographs of this tanks show that this was a short-lived expedient.

2. Some vehicles carried the famous Totenkopf unit insignia on the hull front but this may have been restricted to the company's Pzkpfw III tanks. A later photograph shows a Tiger painted in a very dark colour, possibly a covering of mud, with the marking rendered in white. The oversized stowage boxes used by the two companies mentioned on this page and others are discussed in the Technical Details and Modifications section of this book.

3. Pzkpfw VI ausf H Tiger I. 8.Kompanie, SS-Panzer-Regiment 2. Southern Ukraine, early 1943. The Tigers of this company arrived in Kharkov on 2 February 1943 and were thrown into the defence of the city on the same day. Therefore, it would seem possible that the whitewash camouflage was applied before the tanks left Germany and this would at least account for the very neat appearance of these vehicles evident in almost all the available photographs.The regiment's unit insignia (4) was carried on the hull rear plate (5) and also the left of the hull front near the Kugelblende. Note that the Balkenkreuz features a black outline. Note also the round cover plate, held in place by five support rods, over the exhaust mufflers identifying this tank as a January 1943 production model. This tank was renumbered as 823 and the S24 in April 1943 and took part in battles of Operation Citadel.

INITIAL PRODUCTION
TIGER I
SCHWERE PANZER-ABTEILUNG 502
ANDRES MORA
1/35 SCALE

Venezuelan modeller Andres Mora's replica is based on the Dragon 1/35 scale Initial Production Tiger I with the addition of Friulmodel workable tracks and crew figures from Alpine Miniatures.

Shown below are details of the completed model including the battalion's famous unit insignia, smoke candle dischargers, exhaust mufflers with the extensions commonly seen on tanks of the battalion's 1.Kompanie and the Pzkpfw III stowage box fitted to many of the initial and early production Tigers.

The model was painted in Tamiya acrylics using dark grey and white shades that were progressively diluted with each coat masked off to create the camouflage pattern. The waterslide transfer markings were applied over a coat of Microscale Gloss varnish and then covered in a coating of flat varnish. The extremely impressive weathering was achieved by using washes and filters from Ammo by Mig Jimenez and AK Interactive.

EARLY PRODUCTION
TIGER I
SCHWERE PANZER-ABTEILUNG 503
KONSTANTINOS KALOGEROPOULOS
1/35 SCALE

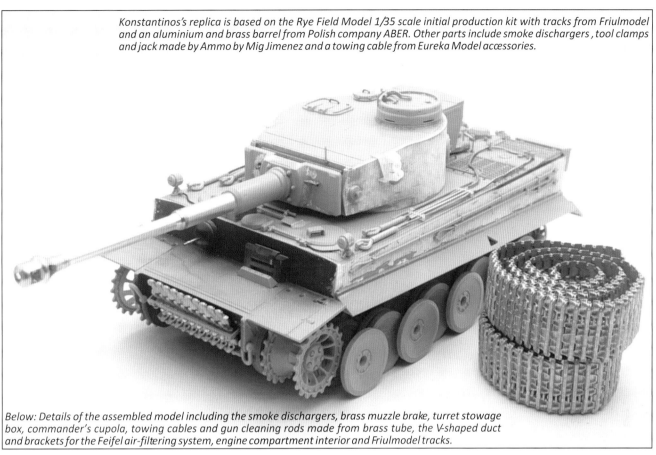

Konstantinos's replica is based on the Rye Field Model 1/35 scale initial production kit with tracks from Friulmodel and an aluminium and brass barrel from Polish company ABER. Other parts include smoke dischargers, tool clamps and jack made by Ammo by Mig Jimenez and a towing cable from Eureka Model accessories.

Below: Details of the assembled model including the smoke dischargers, brass muzzle brake, turret stowage box, commander's cupola, towing cables and gun cleaning rods made from brass tube, the V-shaped duct and brackets for the Feifel air-filtering system, engine compartment interior and Friulmodel tracks.

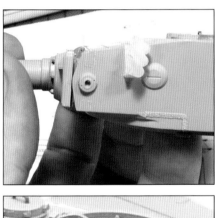

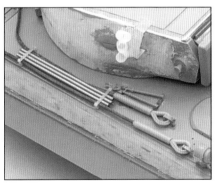

Konstantinos first painted the model in red primer with a dark grey barrel. The component parts of the Tiger I were delivered to the Henschel plant in this primer colour, Rot RAL 8012, and the barrels were coated in a heat-resistant lacquer which was very dark, almost black.

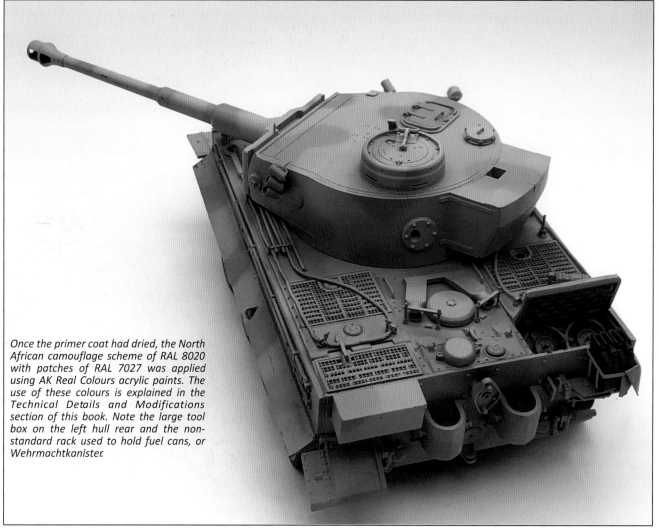

Once the primer coat had dried, the North African camouflage scheme of RAL 8020 with patches of RAL 7027 was applied using AK Real Colours acrylic paints. The use of these colours is explained in the Technical Details and Modifications section of this book. Note the large tool box on the left hull rear and the non-standard rack used to hold fuel cans, or Wehrmachtkanister.

Once the North African camouflage colours had dried very small areas were masked off using masking liquid. This would later assist in the weathering process. The model was then sprayed with white Tamiya acrylic paint to simulate a well-worn coat of whitewash camouflage.

Below: Details of the completed model including the engine deck, exhaust mufflers, hull front and the turret showing the stowage box which was a common feature of this battalion's Tigers, and the pistol port. Note that Konstantinos has not included the Feifel air-filters and their hoses as these were removed from these tanks, probably before they left Germany.

A view of the completed hull and turret. The wheels have been painted but are yet to be weathered. The complex shape of the turret stowage box is clearly shown here.

The completed model with tracks attached. Note the foothold cut into the trackguard just below the Balkenkreuz. This feature is also discussed in the Camouflage & Markings section of this book.

INITIAL PRODUCTION
TIGER I
SCHWERE PANZER-ABTEILUNG 502
NAOMASA DAIRAKU
1/35 SCALE

Naomasa's work has been featured in a number of books in this series and I was very happy to include this model of one of his favourite subjects, the Tiger I, in this project. Naomasa's replica is based on the Dragon Models' 1/35 scale Initial Production kit, shown at right, with many added details and refinements. Shown at the bottom of the page are parts of the partially assembled model including the highly-detailed smoke dischargers, the commander's cupola and the loader's hatch.

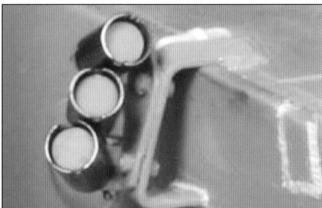

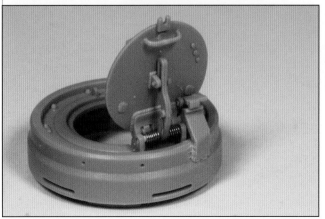

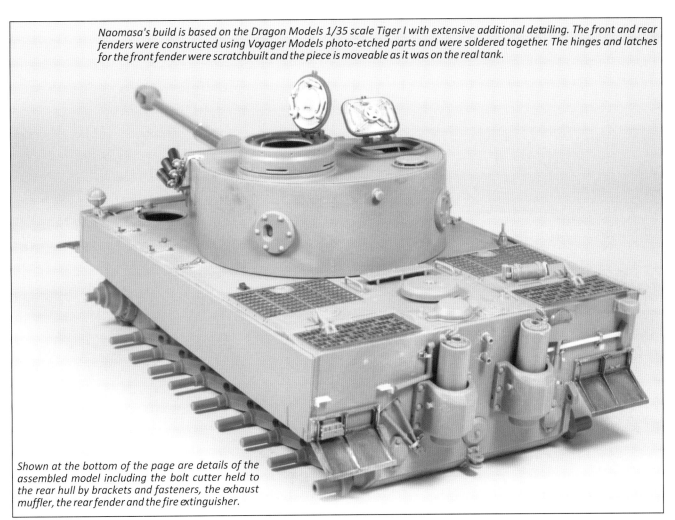

Naomasa's build is based on the Dragon Models 1/35 scale Tiger I with extensive additional detailing. The front and rear fenders were constructed using Voyager Models photo-etched parts and were soldered together. The hinges and latches for the front fender were scratchbuilt and the piece is moveable as it was on the real tank.

Shown at the bottom of the page are details of the assembled model including the bolt cutter held to the rear hull by brackets and fasteners, the exhaust muffler, the rear fender and the fire extinguisher.

The tracks are individual metal links from Master Club and were assembled by inserting resin pins from both sides. Naomasa found it necessary to widen the holes for the pins slightly but the track links were free from flash and burrs and once assembled were fully workable.

When the assembly was completed the model was painted in Gaia Notes German Grey which was lightened with white for scale effect. This lacquer paint has been popular with Japanese modellers for many years and is now available worldwide. To give the mottled appearance evident in photographs of this tank Naomasa lightly sprayed the dark grey base with GSI Creos Mr Color No. 37 Wood Brown and Number 60 IJA Green.

Below: Another view of the completed model. Note the method of attaching the shovel and sledgehammer. At the bottom of the page are shown the Kugelblende machine-gun mount with the toggle bolts on either side, the rear engine deck, the open loader's hatch and details of the commander's cupola and the turret rear with the battalion's charging mammoth unit insignia.

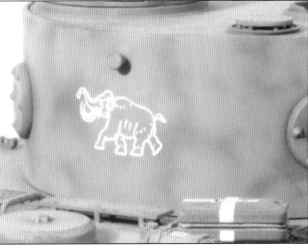

EARLY PRODUCTION
TIGER I
SS-PANZER-REGIMENT 3
THEODOROS KALAMATAS
1/72 SCALE

Theo's work will be familiar to readers of this series and his style and painting techniques, often applied by hand, make for a unique and accurate representation, particularly in these smaller scale offerings. This model is based on the Zvezda 1/72 scale kit and while Theo considered the detail to be adequate, he added scratch-built mesh screens to the engine cooling system on the rear deck and smoke dischargers on the turret sides.

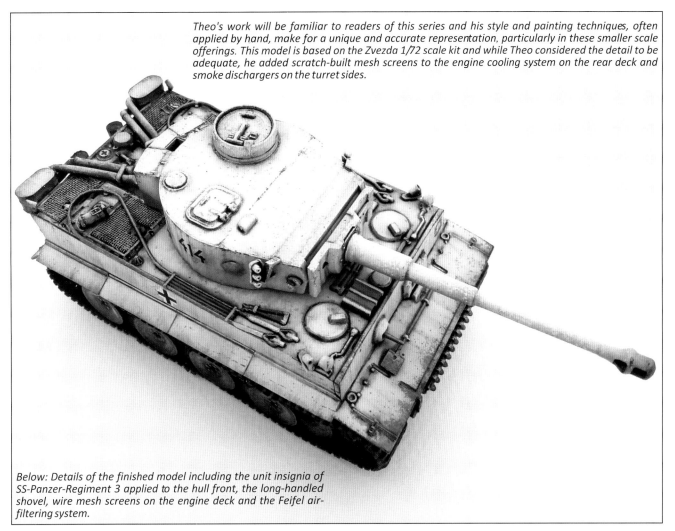

Below: Details of the finished model including the unit insignia of SS-Panzer-Regiment 3 applied to the hull front, the long-handled shovel, wire mesh screens on the engine deck and the Feifel air-filtering system.

The completed model was finished in Tamiya acrylics while the wear and weathering was added using enamel and oil paints from Ammo by Mig Jimenez and AK Interactive.

A rear view of the completed model which shows to good effect the extensive yet realistic weathering. I should mention that Theo accepts commission work and his contact address is listed on page 64.

From the early 1960s, when the first plastic construction kits were released, until today, every major manufacturer, and many smaller companies, have at one time produced scale models of the Tiger I. Most of the early depictions of these deservedly famous tanks would be considered little more than toys today, although many fetch high prices with collectors. In contrast, the more recent models are highly-detailed replicas and additional extras such as photo-etched brass parts, turned aluminium barrels and workable tracks are today commonplace additions. The entry into the market of a number of Chinese manufacturers has also contributed to the proliferation of smaller, specialised companies producing accessories in resin, photo-etched metal, wood and other materials, allowing a level of super-detailing which had previously been the province of a few master modellers. Models of the Tiger are marketed in a number of scales ranging from tiny 6mm wargames miniatures to the large, radio-controlled 1/6 scale versions. But I have chosen to concentrate here, as in the earlier titles, on the most popular modelling scales of 1/35, 1/48 and 1/72 and as the accessory manufacturers have been covered in some detail in the previous titles I have included just a few representative companies. The reader should note that I have not included vehicles or variants which do not fit into the time frame of this book. An index of manufacturers can be found on page 64.

DRAGON MODELS

This Hong Kong-based company's models have become a byword for quality and accuracy and the extensive catalogue is probably only matched by Tamiya. Currently Dragon Models offer a large number of Tiger I variants in 1/35 and 1/72 scale including kits of the Bergetiger recovery vehicle. From time to time many of these models are repackaged with bonus items such as photo-etched parts or new sets of markings under the Cyberhobby label. Most of the 1/35 scale offerings have also been released in 1/72 scale, as either construction kits or pre-painted replicas, and the company produces a number of assembled and pre-painted models in 1/144 scale.

Above, left to right: Dragon Models' 1/35 scale early production Tiger I. The company's second version of the initial production version, also in 1/35 scale. The latter also contains parts to build Tiger 100 shown on page 17 of the Camouflage & Markings section.

At right: Dragon Models' early production 1/35 scale replica built following the kit instructions. Although the model shown on the box above depicts a tank at the time of Operation Citadel, this vehicle was actually one of the original allocation made to SS-Panzer-Regiment 2.

TAMIYA INCORPORATED

This Japanese company has been manufacturing plastic kits since 1959, releasing their first armour model two years later. By the early 1970s Tamiya was producing a large range of armoured vehicles and accessories and the company was almost solely responsible for the rise in popularity of 1/35 scale. Like Airfix, the adoption of a constant scale proved popular at a time when many manufacturers were making models to fit the box in which they would eventually be marketed. In 2003 Tamiya began releasing a series of models in 1/48 scale, a size which had largely been forgotten until then, and this line has been extremely successful for the company. At the time of writing Tamiya produces early and mid production versions of the Tiger I in 1/35 scale, and an early production variant in 1/48 scale. Tamiya also offers an impressive 1/16 scale radio-controlled early production Tiger and the 1/35 scale versions have at various times been made as motorised replicas.

At left: Tamiya's early production Tiger I in 1/48 scale built with the photo-etched brass and resin upgrade set form Eduard Model Accessories. Note that the spare track links and the brackets that hold them to the turret sides were not introduced into production until April 1943 and therefore slightly outside the period covered by this book.

RYE FIELD MODELS

A relatively new model company based in Hong Kong, Rye Field Models has released three kits depicting Tiger I variants all in the short space of time between September 2015 and February 2016. The initial production model depicts a Tiger with the modifications seen on the first tanks sent to Tunisia and the early production version features extensive interior detailing. Contrary to what has been written elsewhere, these are not re-worked or re-issued kits but completely new models.

At left: Rye Field Models' early production Tiger I. This model features photo-etched parts with fully workable tracks and suspension. The turret stowage box is correct for just a small number of tanks assembled in December 1942, perhaps as few as nine, and allocated to schwere Panzer-Abteilung 503.

Above: Rye Field Models' early production Tiger I which actually represents one of the Tigers sent to North Africa. At left: The choice of gun mantlets that comes with the Tiger I kit.

ZVEZDA

Founded in 1990, this Russian company's catalogue is heavily weighted towards modern Russian and Soviet-era vehicle and aircraft models but does include an early production model Tiger I in 1/35 scale which is a retooling of an older kit first released in 1996. The same version is also offered in 1/72 and 1/100 scale, the latter size being roughly compatible with 15mm wargames figures.

At left: Zvezda's early production 1/72 scale Tiger I model. This version is also produced in 1/100 scale in an almost identical box. Below: The Zvezda 1/35 scale early production Tiger I built with photo-etched brass details from Eduard Model Accessories.

HOBBY FAN/AFV CLUB

Hobby Fan Enterprises is the parent company of AFV Club, both of which are based in Taiwan. Most kits feature non-standard inclusions such as turned metal gun barrels, photo-etched brass parts and water-slide transfers offering numerous schemes. The 1/48 scale early production Tiger I model formally produced by Skybow is now marketed under the AFV Club logo. An example of this model can also be seen in the Model Showcase section from page 27. The company also provides accessories in the shape of both solid plastic and workable tracks for the Tiger I in both 1/35 and 1/48 scale in addition to ammunition, wooden crates and other general items.

At left: The narrow Tiger I transport tracks in 1/35 scale. Below: AFV Club's 1/48 scale early-production Tiger I, formerly marketed by Skybow. Although this model is finished in the markings of SS-Panzer-Regiment 2 at the time of the Kursk battles, this vehicle was with the regiment in the first months of 1943.

ACADEMY PLASTIC MODELS

Based in Korea, this company's Military Miniatures range of 1/35 scale figures and vehicles includes an early, mid and late production Tiger I. The early production model was originally released in 1996 and has since been issued in several different incarnations, sometimes with additional parts or new markings. The example shown below is the 1997 version with full interior detailing. Others include kits with upgraded parts and marking options for Tigers that were in service during Operation Citadel and a tank with crew figures dressed in winter uniforms.

At right: Academy's 1/35 scale early production Tiger I. Although this model is marketed as a vehicle which took part in Operation Citadel with SS-Panzer-Regiment 2, the smoke dischargers had been removed by that time and this replica is in fact closer to the January 1943 incarnation when Tiger S13 was numbered 811.

MODEL FACTORY HIRO

This Japanese company is probably best known for its highly-detailed multi-media racing car and motorcycle kits and their foray into armour modelling was spectacular if short-lived. The company's early production Tiger I was first released as a limited-edition kit in 2013 and that was followed within twelve months by a late production version, both in 1/35 scale. Both models featured extensive interior detailing and were made from resin, white metal and aluminium as well as photo-etched brass. The tracks and suspension were fully workable and each kit contained a comprehensive sheet of water-slide transfers. The company's boast that these were the most accurate models of the Tiger to be produced fell somewhat short but they were an extremely brave attempt and although both are currently out of production I have included them here as limited numbers of these complex and expensive models are released from time to time.

Below: Model Factory Hiro's 1/35 scale early production Tiger I after complete assembly. At right: Details of the turret and hull interior. In addition to the materials mentioned above the kit has parts made from glass fibre and UV photopolymer.

ROCHM MODEL

Rochm Model is the brainchild of modeller Sheng Hui whose work has appeared in a number of books in the TankCraft series. Initially specialising in detail sets in resin, photo-etched brass and aluminium for the Tiger I, the company moved onto the Tiger II and Panther and now offers a 3D printing service for 1/35 and 1/16 scale models. The numerous upgrade sets for the Tiger I include photo-etched brass details which are intended to build actual tanks at specific times in their operational life, for example Tiger Fgst Nr.250049 of SS-Panzer-Regiment 2 and an initial production vehicle of schwere Panzer-Abteilung 502. These products offer exceptional detail and considering the quality are reasonably priced. Although the catalogue is heavily slanted towards Dragon Model kits, these details would be suitable for most 1/35 scale models.

Below, right: Dragon Models' initial production Tiger I in 1/35 scale completed with the photo-etched brass and resin set from Rochm.

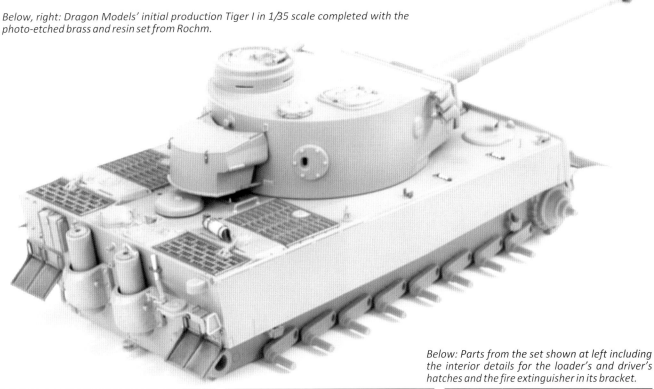

Below: Parts from the set shown at left including the interior details for the loader's and driver's hatches and the fire extinguisher in its bracket.

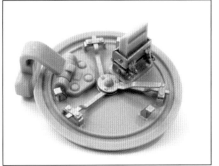
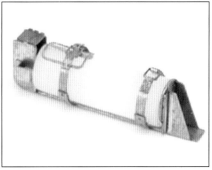

ROYAL MODELS

This Italian company has been producing high quality accessories and aftermarket parts since the early 1990s under the guidance of its founder, Roberto Reale. The catalogue includes complete upgrade sets in 1/35 scale for the early, mid and late production Tiger I and a limited number of sets in 1/72 and 1/48 scale. Royal Models also offers a number of realistic crew figures for the larger-scale models. Shown here are the Feifel air filters of the early production kits (1), turret stowage bin (2) and headlight, hatch interior detail and tools (3), all in 1/35 scale.

ABER

This Polish company has been manufacturing and selling upgrade sets since 1995 working in photo-etched brass, milled aluminium and brass, stainless steel and even wood. A full list of the accessories made specifically for the Tiger in all scales would be far too large to reproduce in this book and the reader can find the company's contact details on page 64. The images shown here are, from left to right, part of the 1/35 scale upgrade set for the early production Tigers that served in Tunisia, photo-etched brass details for the Feifel air filters and the early pattern muzzle brake for the L/56 gun.

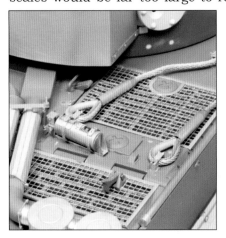  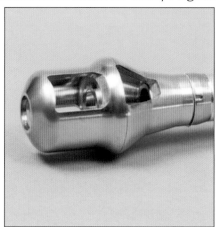

E.T. MODEL

This Shanghai-based company produces highly-detailed upgrade sets in 1/72 and 1/35 scale in brass, aluminium and resin. The range covers not only military subjects but also exquisitely detailed diorama accessories such as garden furniture. The models of Penny Shi, who works as a designer at E.T. Model, have been featured in this series. Most sets are designed, according to the company, to fit specific kits but some, for example the turret stowage bin and towing cables, are referred to as universal. Of particular interest for this study, the company offers comprehensive detail sets for the initial and early production versions in both 1/72 and 1/35 scale.

Below: Dragon Models' 1/72 scale initial production Tiger I built with E.T. Model's resin and photo-etched detail brass set.

Below, left to right: Resin roadwheel flanges. Photo-etched and resin details for the initial production Tiger I. Parts of the photo-etched brass set for the early production Tiger I. All in 1/35 scale.

In 1937 the Heereswaffenamt, the German army's weapons procurement and development office, asked the firm of Henschel und Sohn of Kassel to design a tank in the 30 to 33-ton class that would eventually replace the Pzkpfw IV medium tank which was just then entering service. Christened Durchbruchswagen, or breakthrough tank, the first proposal was essentially a Pzkpfw III hull with a Pzkpfw IV turret fitted with a 7.5cm L/24 gun. Just one example of Durchbruchswagen I was completed before work began on Durchbruchswagen II, a still heavier design, and although the project was officially shelved in 1938, a number of features influenced future projects.

Through the last months of peace and into 1940, Henschel, Daimler-Benz, Porsche and MAN worked on the development of entirely new designs for medium and heavy tanks which would utilise the Schachtellaufwerk torsion bar suspension system which was made up overlapping and interleaved road wheels. This arrangement was a significant departure from the system of roadwheels supported on double bogies which characterised German tank development up to that time.

The battles of 1940 had shown that the Pzkpfw IV, the heaviest German tank then in service, was at a decided disadvantage when confronted with the French Char B and British Matilda II but the campaign had been such a spectacular success that weapons development slipped lower on the scale of priorities. Tasked with almost doubling the number of Panzer battalions in preparation for the invasion of the Soviet Union the army focused on production. But in June 1941 the Wehrmacht was suddenly confronted with armoured vehicles which combined thick, sloped armour with mobility and firepower.

The shock caused by the first encounters with the Russian T-34 and KV series of heavy tanks cannot be underestimated and Hitler demanded that while development of the Schachtellaufwerk designs continue, work begin immediately on a still heavier vehicle with armour that would withstand any anti-tank gun then in use. In addition, the proposed tank was to have the capability of destroying any enemy tank at ranges of 1,500 metres and to achieve this a tapered-bore gun firing a tungsten-core projectile, an innovation for its day, was to be fitted.

This weapon would have more than adequately fulfilled the role but the supply of tungsten could not be guaranteed and the only other comparable weapon was the 8.8cm KwK36 which was based on the Flak 18 anti-aircraft gun. In the production version of the Tiger I this gun was fitted with the T.Z.F.9b sight manufactured by Ernst Leitz of Wetzlar which endowed the weapon with exceptional accuracy (1). Working day and night, the designers and engineers at Henschel and Porsche succeeded in completing prototypes in under a year and both were transported by rail to Hitler's headquarters at Rastenburg in East Prussia, arriving on 19 April 1942 (2).

Notes

1. In trials conducted during the war by the British army using a captured Tiger, the 8.8cm gun was able to consistently hit a 1-metre square stationary target at ranges of over 1,000 metres. The rate of accuracy was only diminished when the target was moving and obscured by smoke.

2. The deadline had been imposed on both companies so that the prototypes could be view by Hitler on his birthday, 20 April.

Fgst Nr. V1, the first Henschel prototype photographed in April 1942 at the company's Kassel assembly plant. This vehicle had several features which were not included on the production models including the Vorpanzer spaced armour (A) which could be pivoted forward and down to offer additional protection to the front plate. Although it was very quickly rejected a number of initial production tanks retained modifications to the hull front extensions that would have allowed for the fitting of the Vorpanzer shield. Note also the snorkel (B) for submersible running installed in its socket on the engine deck. Just visible is a horn (C) which was also not mounted on the production vehicles.

Captured by the Russians on 18 January 1943, this initial production Tiger I was one of four tanks sent to the Eastern Front in August 1942 with 1.Kompanie, schwere Panzer-Abteilung 502. The battalion's unit insignia is just visible on the rear of the turret. A number of fittings are missing including the 15-ton jack, which would have been held in the brackets on the right side of the hull rear plate, and the right side stowage bin. The metal beams which held the latter in place are still attached. Note that the pistol port has apparently been removed and replaced in the wrong position with the aperture facing forward.

Notes

1. The Henschel vehicle had actually been built in two versions, the H1, which was fitted with the 8.8cm gun, and the H2 which was armed with a 7.5cm weapon.

2. Speaking after the war, the Henschel designers admitted that they had been able to persuade Speer, and through him Hitler, that manoeuvrability was a key factor.

The Henschel design received the official classification VK 4501(H) while the Porsche prototype was referred to as VK 4501 (P) and while both utilised the same turret, the hull and suspension layouts were markedly different (1). The turret and gun of both prototypes was designed by Friedrich Krupp AG of Essen in consultation with the engineers at Porsche, originally for the company's Typ 100 Leopard.

As the Porsche tank was offloaded from its rail car it immediately sank into the soft ground and, despite several attempts, it could not be extricated under its own power.

Dr Ferdinand Porsche, who accompanied the prototype, is supposed to have been approached by Erwin Anders, Henschel's chief designer, who offered to have his tank tow the Porsche vehicle free. If this story is true it was very much an idle boast on Anders' part as both tanks crawled the final 11 kilometres to Rastenburg, breaking down continuously and having to be nursed through the entire length of the journey.

On the following day both prototype tanks were presented to Hitler and put through their paces. In many respects the Porsche vehicle proved the be the most impressive, but both Hitler and Speer, his armaments minister, were swayed by the superior manoeuvrability displayed by the Henschel prototype, just as its designers knew they would be and it was ordered into production (2). As 100 hulls and turrets had already been ordered for the

Porsche design from Krupp it was anticipated that these would go into service, specifically with schwere Panzer-Abteilungen 501 and 503, but design problems and lagging production had convinced Hitler by November 1942 that Henschel should be the sole manufacturer of the Tiger and the Porsche programme was officially terminated in the same month. Just one completed vehicle saw combat as a Befehlspanzerwagen with Panzerjäger-Abteilung 653 and was destroyed in July 1944 on the Eastern Front. The hulls were used in the Panzerjäger Elefant/Ferdinand project.

The Henschel production vehicle consisted of an armoured hull, or Panzerwanne, made up of a fighting compartment, a closed engine compartment and two side panniers. The latter were necessary to accommodate the width of the Krupp turret. The turret drive, steering gear, brakes, transmission, driver's and radio operator's positions, hull machine gun and the complete ammunition stowage for the 8.8cm gun were located in the fighting compartment. The driver's front plate and front nose plate were of 100mm thickness while the glacis was of 60mm thickness but angled to provide greater protection. The superstructure side plates and hull side plates, behind the wheels, were of 80mm and 60mm thickness respectively. A machine-gun ball mount, or Kugelblende, was inset into the driver's front plate in front of the radio operator's position. To support the Tiger's weight the suspension was constructed as a so-called Schachtellaufwerk where the road wheels were interleaved. The outer row of road wheels could be easily removed to facilitate rail transport by reducing the overall vehicle width and sets of narrow tracks were also provided. A fully traversable turret was mounted centrally on the hull deck and this contained the main gun and a machine gun. The turret roof contained a forward-opening hatch for the loader and a cylindrical cupola for the commander. On the hull deck, in front of the turret, were hatches for the driver and radio operator. The fully-assembled chassis, incorporating the Panzerwanne and suspension, were identified by a unique number which was referred to as a Fahrgestellnummer (Fgst Nr.) and the Tiger I series began with 250001. The turrets were manufactured by Wegmann & Co., and transported to the Henschel plant, just over a kilometre away, where the final assembly took place. Each turret was also identified by an individual number, here referred to as a Turm Nr, and these began at 1 (1).

The Tiger I engines were produced by Maybach of Friedrichshafen and the main guns, the famous 8.8cm KwK 36 L/56, were assembled by Dortmund Hoerder Hüttenverein and R. Wolf AG at their Magdeberg-Buchau factory.

The first production models were referred to as Panzerkampfwagen VI H (8.8cm) ausf H1, with the ordnance designation SdKfz 182, and the title Tiger I is not encountered in official documentation until October 1942, probably to differentiate the tank from the Tiger II project which by then in the early planning stages. On 27 February 1943 a personal order from Hitler directed that the tank should henceforth be referred to as the Panzerkampfwagen Tiger ausf E SdKfz 181 and this designation remained in force until the end of the war. As a matter of convenience I have referred to the tank as Pzkpfw VI ausf H or Tiger I throughout this book.

In August 1942 the first production Tiger tanks to see combat left the assembly lines at the massive Henschel und Sohn plant at Kassel in western Germany and it should be said that the eight tanks completed during that month, including the four vehicles of 1.Kompanie, schwere Panzer-Abteilung 502 operating near Leningrad, were essentially at the prototype stage. Many modifications were made during the assembly of subsequent vehicles and the most important of these are listed below. A number of these, particularly field modifications, are also highlighted in the Camouflage & Markings section. But I should mention that as the purpose of this chapter is to enable the reader to confidently determine when a particular tank was manufactured, the many internal changes are for the most part not listed. It should also be noted that the terms initial and early production are modern inventions and were not in use during the war.

Notes

1. This is a simplified explanation of what is a rather complicated system which is explained further in the production and allocation tables presented on pages 62 and 63.

This early production Tiger I of 1.Kompanie, schwere Panzer-Abteilung 503 was photographed during the fighting for Kharkov and may have been one of the tanks finished in the North Africa camouflage colours with patches of Dunkelgrau RAL 7021 as discussed in the Camouflage & Markings section of this book. Features to note are the Pzkpfw III stowage box, the early pattern hull track guards, smoke candle dischargers, brackets for the long-handled shovel on the glacis and early style hull extensions.

Below: An initial production Tiger I assembled in August 1942. Note the angle of the hull front extensions, the method of welding the hull side plates, the bent front fender attached to the hull by hinges, the exhaust mufflers and the lack of brackets on the hull side to hold the track changing cable. Note also the fixtures to hold a turret stowage box behind the pistol port.

April 1942. Fgst Nr. V1, the first of three test vehicles, was completed and accepted by the Heereswaffenamt. It was delivered to Kraftfahrversuchstelle Kummersdorf, the army's automotive proving ground, in May. Henschel had originally been contracted to build 100 VK 4501(H) chassis, beginning with Fgst Nr.250001, but during this month a further order was placed for an additional 200 vehicles to be completed as Pzkpfw VI H ausf H2, equipped with the 7.5cm L/70 gun.

May 1942. Beginning with Fgst Nr. 250001, periscopes with protective armour covers were installed in the driver's and radio operator's hatches. It was decided that the Vorpanzer shield of the prototype vehicle should not be incorporated into production and the holes for the pivoting arms were either cut away or plugged. These modifications were still visible on a small number of initial production vehicles as a number of hulls had been completed in anticipation of the Vorpanzer being fitted.

The hull glacis, where it covered the tracks, was cut off and bent metal track guards, mounted on hinges, were added. Frames were welded to the rear hull to hold rear track guards. The horn, mounted on the hull between the driver's and loader's hatches of the V1 prototype

vehicle, was not fitted to the production models. Henschel had planned to assemble three Tigers in this month but just one vehicle was completed.

June 1942. Instructions were provided by the Heereswaffenamt (HWA) for mounting smoke candle dischargers, or Nebelwurfgerät, on each side of the turret towards the front. Although the brackets to hold these were fitted from August 1942 the dischargers were not available until the following October. None of the planned five Tigers was completed in this month.

July 1942. The plan to mount the 7.5cm L/70 in 200 production vehicles was abandoned and the 8.8cm L/56 gun was adopted as standard. On 5 July the management at Henschel advised that problems with the steering gear, transmission and brakes had still not been resolved but they were confident that the production target for August 1942 could be met.

August 1942. The driver's twin periscope was dropped from production and the two holes drilled in the hull glacis above the visor were welded shut. A hinged flap was installed on the top of each muffler to keep out water during submerged fording and retaining hooks were added to the engine louvres. Fasteners were welded to the rear deck to hold five gun cleaning rods and

............continued on page 54

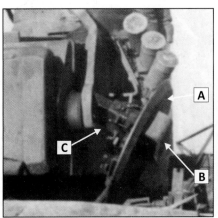
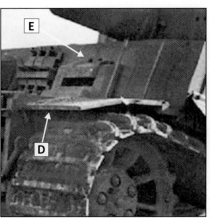

Above, from left to right: A. The driver's hatch in the open position showing the armour cover (B) and periscope (C). The radio operator's hatch on the right-hand side was a mirror image of this. In the background can be seen the smoke candle dischargers, here with their rubber covers in place, and the bracket which held them to the turret side. D. The initial design bent metal fender and apertures for the early driver's periscope (E). F. The same apertures after being welded shut.

Probably the most distinctive feature of the initial and early production Tiger I tanks was the cylindrical commander's cupola. Shown here is a tank of 13.Kompanie, Panzer-Regiment Grossdeutchland and although this photograph was taken in the late spring of 1943, slightly later than the period covered by our study, it shows a number of details that are often not clear in other images. A. The hatch locking handles. The cupola hatch had a watertight seal. B. Part of the latch. C. The rain cover support. D. A short piece of wire was welded in front of the forward-facing periscope aperture (E) to provide a basic vane sight. A similar piece was welded to the inside. F. Drainage holes. These were angled downwards. G. The spring-loaded hatch locking bar. H. Metal arm welded to the cupola side which held the hatch at the angle shown here. I. 18mm diameter metal handle.

............continued from page 52

Notes

1. The term early production is used today to describe tanks that left the assembly line after August 1942 and before late July 1943 when the cast commander's cupola was introduced into production with Turm Nr.391 and Fgst Nr. 250391.

two wrecking bars. A storage tube for a spare antenna was mounted along the outside edge of the hull at the right rear. Holes were cut into the glacis plate at each corner to accommodate a canvas cover intended to disguise the tank as a truck. It is not known if these were ever used.

Although the need for external stowage had been realised as early as June 1942, when a contract had been awarded to Vorrichtungs und Gerätebau GmbH to design a Gepächkasten specifically for the Henschel prototype, the first Tigers allocated to schwere Panzer-Abteilung 502 had no stowage box. An unknown number of these were fitted with the field-modified version shown on page 17 of the Camouflage & Markings section and in the photograph on page 9. It was some time until the purpose-built boxes were available and it is likely that the remainder of the August production run and most of the vehicles assembled in September and October were fitted with a Pzkpfw III stowage box.

Just eight Tigers were assembled in August and these tanks, with Fgst Nr. 250001, are referred to today as the initial production models (1).

September 1942. The two toggle bolts on the machine-gun mount were no longer installed. From Fgst Nr.250011 fasteners were installed on the left hull side to hold the track replacement cable. Fasteners were also added to hold a hammer, spade, axe, wooden jack block, wire cutters, a wrecking bar, two towing cables and a fire extinguisher on the rear deck. A 15-ton jack was fitted vertically to the rear hull.

On 10 September Henschel was directed to install a Kampfraumbeheizung, or crew compartment heater. This consisted of a sheet metal housing which fed warm air from the cooling exhaust into the fighting compartment. These may have entered production in November, or perhaps later, and were present on the tanks sent to southern Ukraine in late 1942 and early 1943. They were all removed by their crews who feared that the restriction of any airflow would cause a fire and they are very rarely seen in photographs.

October 1942. Three smoke candle dischargers, or Nebelwurfgerät, were fitted on the turret sides towards the front. Mounting plates for the Feifel air filters were incorporated into production but the filters themselves were not fitted until

Above: The evolution of the Tiger I turret stowage box. A. The first four tanks of 1.Kompanie, schwere Panzer-Abteilung 502 sent to the Leningrad Front had no stowage boxes and at least one was fitted with a field-modified version on both sides of the turret. B. The available photographs show that most, if not all, the other tanks of the company were given stowage boxes designed for the Pzkpfw III tank. The position of the box seen here was indicative of this battalion. C. Tigers of schwere Panzer-Abteilung 503 were also fitted with the Pzkpfw III stowage box, attached much higher on the turret. D. A number of tanks of schwere Panzer-Abteilung 503 were rushed to the front in December and these were fitted with the stowage box shown here. The container on the left side and fire extinguisher were much later additions. E. An example of the early, much oversized, stowage box here cut to fit over the pistol port. This tank is from SS-Panzer-Regiment 1. F. The standard stowage box introduced into production from February 1943.

Below: An early production Tiger I assembled in February 1942. This tank features the early drive sprocket which was dropped from production in April 1943, the dischargers for the smoke candles or Nebelwurfgeräte on the turret side introduced from

from October 1942, hinged fenders at front and rear and the straight-sided track guards. This vehicle would also have been fitted with the brackets for S-Mine dischargers although the dischargers themselves were not yet available. Note the Feifel air-filtration system which was introduced into production from October 1942 and the oversized stowage bin, or Gepäckkasten, held here with a single metal beam on each side.

November 1942. Beginning with Fgst Nr.250021, standardised cross-country tracks, referred to as Kgs 63/725/130, were fitted to both sides. The first twenty Tigers were fitted with left and right cross-country tracks which were not interchangeable.

The rectangular convoy light was replaced by a cylindrical model and the antenna base on the hull rear was removed. The position of the towing cables on the deck was reversed and the 15-ton jack was mounted horizontally. Beginning with Fgst Nr.250031, fasteners were fixed to the glacis to hold a long-handled shovel. This modification was continued until January 1944.

The first version of the large, purpose-built stowage box may have been introduced into production in this month. It is known they were fitted to the Tigers of schwere Panzer-Abteilung 501, replacing the Pzkpfw III models, before 2.Kompanie left for North Africa. It must be assumed that these boxes were not mounted in the factory as they did not fit the turrets correctly, interfering with the pistol ports. The design was altered after about twenty examples had been produced but these also proved to be too large and with the introduction of the hinged escape hatch in

December 1942 the problem was only exacerbated. Several units, all depicted in the Camouflage & Markings section, found different ways to adapt the boxes to their tank's turrets.

November 1942. Thin sheet metal mudguards, sometimes referred to as track guards, were fitted to the hull sides and hinged fenders were added at the front. The track guards consisted of four sections, mounted in pairs, at an angle, so as to create a slight dip in the middle join. Initially, each section was constructed by welding a thin upper retaining strip to a lower guard strip but from sometime after Fgst Nr.250028 they were fabricated from a single piece of metal.

A canvas rain shield for the commander's cupola was introduced. This was held by a wire frame that slotted into metal support sleeves on the cupola sides. Sprung counterbalances were added to both the loader's and commander's hatch covers. A number of tanks were built with reinforced main gun mantlets.

December 1942. The sheet metal track guards were fitted in a straight line whereas previously they had followed the curve of the lower edge of the hull side. An escape hatch, or Notausstiegluke, was

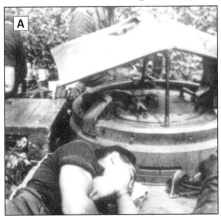

Above, from left to right: A. The canvas rain cover in place over the commander's cupola. Note the two sockets, welded to the cupola, which hold the metal frame. B. The reinforced gun mantlet introduced into production in November 1942. This was only applied to the left side of the mantlet, in front of the gunner's position, and not the right side as it would have interfered with the already-limited traverse of the turret machine gun. C. The escape hatch on the right side of the turret which replaced the pistol port in December 1942. This photograph also shows the method adopted by SS-Panzer-Regiment 2 to fit the early, oversized stowage boxes.

installed in the right rear turret side in place of the pistol port. It is believed that the shape of the first production hatches conformed to the curvature of the turret sides but by July 1943 a flat disc shape was in use. From Fgst Nr.250053, reinforcing rings were added to the holes for the canvas camouflage cover.

From Fgst Nr.250055 the hull sides were extended at the front which allowed the U-shaped towing shackles to pivot. A small stowage box for the track tools was fitted to the hull rear plate above the left track guard. Mounts for five S-Mine dischargers were fixed to the hull roof, although the dischargers themselves were not available until January, and the antenna stowage tube was moved to accommodate the S-Mine mount. The Tigers allocated to schwere Panzer-Abteilung 503 in this month left the factory without a number of standard fittings including turret stowage boxes. A special box was fabricated, possibly by the base workshops at Fallingbostel, and an example is shown on page 21 of the Camouflage & Markings section. At least one Tiger of 4.Kompanie, SS-Panzer-Regiment 3 was also fitted with one of these boxes.

January 1943. Ninety Tigers were assembled with gun mantlets originally intended for the cancelled VK 4501 (P) project. Unlike the mantlets introduced in November 1942, these did not have the reinforced casting over the gun sight aperture. A sheet metal guard or deflector was fitted to the open sides of the mufflers to conceal the distinctive glow given off by the exhausts. Beginning with Fgst Nr.250082 five S-Mine dischargers were fitted on the hull roof with one at each corner and one mounted halfway along the left side. The fifth discharger was not fitted to the Panzerbefehlswagen variant. From Fgst Nr.250085, triangular support sections were welded to the ends of each hull track guard. From Fgst Nr.250101, locking strips were fitted to the roadwheels to better secure the bolts. A total of thirty-five completed vehicles left the assembly lines at Henschel in this month, the highest number achieved so far.

February 1943. From Fgst Nr.250122 the number of gun cleaning rods was increased to six and fasteners to hold the engine hand-cranked starter were fitted to the lower left of the hull rear plate. To reinforce the roadwheels, two smaller diameter bolts were added for each original bolt giving a total of eighteen. In early February, or possibly late January, a new turret stowage box was introduced replacing the ill-fitting earlier version.

March 1943. A fixed loader's periscope, protected by an armoured cover, was installed on the turret roof beginning with Turm Nr.184. Modified Feifel air filters were introduced and the cap over the ventilation riser on the rear deck was replaced by a triangular-shaped opening covered by a flat plate held in place by three bolts. Track pins retained by a ring were fitted from Fgst Nr.250145.

Assembled in November or December 1942, prior to Fgst Nr. 250055, this early production Tiger I of 2.Kompanie, schwere Panzer-Abteilung 503 survived over 250 hits by Russian tank and anti-tank guns during the battles of January 1943. It was returned to Germany for repair but it was found that only the turret could be salvaged. This vehicle exhibits several interesting features of the tanks allocated to the battalion before 1943 including the early hull extensions, the pistol port on the right side of the turret and the early loader's hatch. Note that the driver's visor has been removed. This tank, in an earlier incarnation, is shown on page 24 of the Camouflage & Markings section.

Until quite recently it was generally believed that during the early war period all German military vehicles were painted in an overall shade of very dark grey, sometimes referred to as Schwartzgrau or Panzergrau (1).

In February 1943 this was superseded by a much lighter colour called Dunkelgelb, or dark yellow, which was to be applied to all vehicles before they left the factories. Units in the field were supplied with red-brown and green paint which could be sprayed or brushed over the Dunkelgelb base coat to create a pattern of camouflage. Whitewash, which could be easily removed, was supplied during the winter months.

More in-depth research has shown that this view is far too simplistic and as the time period covered by this book takes us neatly up to the introduction of a standard camouflage for all fronts we should take the opportunity to examine the subject in some detail.

Although the following explanation is rather lengthy it will provide the reader with an understanding of what is a complex subject during a time of transition. In addition, the developments mentioned here are relevant to the other books in this series and future titles.

Two of the most important factors governing German armoured vehicles are the various Heeresmitteilungen, or army orders, and the RAL colour system.

Allgemeine Heeresmitteilungen, or general army orders, were disseminated twice each month and were used to announce significant measures including changes to uniform regulations, awards, discipline, training methods, replacements and even the morale of the troops. Most importantly for our study they stipulated the colours and methods by which vehicles, guns and buildings were to be painted. In addition, Heeres-Verordnungsblatt (HVT) were issued to advise of less important changes and indicative of their mostly mundane nature was the fact that these documents were not considered restricted material as Heeresmitteilungen were.

The RAL was set up in 1925 under the auspices of a number of large business concerns and government authorities (2). The commission was entrusted with the regulation of various standards of practice and manufacturing and in 1927 adopted a colour coding system referred to as RAL 840.

Whereas it had previously been necessary to provide samples or colour swatches to a paint manufacturer, who would then attempt to recreate the colour and shade, it was now possible to obtain an exact match by quoting a RAL 840 reference, for example Dunkelgrau 46 (3). As originally conceived, RAL 840 consisted of just forty different shades but was expanded and modified somewhat in 1933 to become RAL 840 B2. But by 1940 the range of

Notes

1. Schwartzgrau is included in the present-day RAL system but the term Panzergrau is a modern invention. The correct term for the 1939-1945 period is Dunkelgrau.
2. Reichs-Ausschuss für Lieferbedingungen und Gütesicherung or the Commission for Delivery Terms and Quality Assurance.
3. This, it should be remembered, is an exact match by the standards of 1927.

Above: Photographed in May 1943 at Henschel's Kassel plant, the Tiger I in the foreground is Fgst Nr. 250234, the fourth tank completed in that month. The spare track link brackets on the turret side, the machined drive sprocket and, just visible on the turret roof, the loader's periscope were all modifications introduced in April 1943. Although slightly outside the period examined by this study I have included this image to illustrate the high contrast between Dunkelgelb RAL 7028 and some of the darker finishes. Tiger Fgst Nr. 250238 in the background is almost certainly coated in Rot RAL 8012, the primer with which all parts were initially painted and although dark it is significantly lighter than freshly-applied RAL 7021 Dunkelgrau.

A Pzkpfw III ausf A and Pzkpfw IV ausf A painted in the early-war camouflage pattern consisting of a Dunkelgrau 46 base coat with disruptive patches of Dunkelbraun 45. Note that the tarpaulins of the trucks in the background have been similarly treated. Although this scheme was widespread it is often very difficult to discern in monochrome photographs due to the low contrast between the two colours.

Notes

1. Surviving images where the edges of a darker colour are visible probably depict vehicles repainted after November 1938.

2. The date of this order is given in some sources as 31 June 1940 but a surviving copy clearly shows the July date.

colours had grown to become so unwieldy that the system was completely reorganised and renamed RAL Farbtonregister 840-R. Each colour was given a four-digit number with the first digit generally indicating the shade, for example Grau RAL 7027 and Dunkelgrau 7021. The system underwent further changes between 1953 and 1961 and emerged as RAL 840-HR and today includes thousands of colours. It should be borne in mind that although certain numbers and names have been retained, many now describe colours which are significantly different to those used during the war and some codes bear no relationship to the colours they described in 1945.

Throughout the Polish and French campaigns many tanks were painted in accordance with a practice that began with Heeresmitteilung (HM) Nr.340 dated 12 July 1937, but later ratified by HM Nr.687 of 2 November 1938, which stipulated the use of Dunkelbraun 45 painted over a base coat of Dunkelgrau 46, the former covering approximately one-third of the surface area. Units were expected to acquire the paint from commercial sources and a list of approved companies was included with the order. The 1937 instruction directed that the camouflage was to be rendered with soft or feathered edges but the 1938 document makes no mention of the method of application (1).

Given that the contrast between Dunkelbraun 45 and Dunkelgrau 46 is almost non-existent in most monochrome

photographs it is hardly surprising that this scheme was largely ignored by many authors and researchers and that the proposition of a single dark colour being used throughout this period was accepted as fact.

Most early works on German camouflage colours relied on the information contained in Fritz Wiener's *Der Anstrich des Heeresgerätes 1939-1945*, originally compiled in 1957.

Herr Wiener's report mentioned the use of a colour he described as a dark grey-brown being employed after 1935 but his research uncovered no official orders prior to the July 1940 directive that all military vehicles would henceforth be painted in a single colour. To be fair to Wiener, his research was conducted at a time when almost no secondary evidence existed and many primary documents were stored in Eastern Bloc countries.

Somewhat more difficult to understand is the error included in the 1967 English language version, produced by the Bovington Tank Museum, where Wiener's 1940 date is incorrectly transcribed as July 1939. In fact, the practice of using a single colour was not standardised until the dissemination of HM Nr.864 dated 31 July 1940, issued after the conclusion of the French campaign, and although it is only implied in the original document we can assume that colour was Dunkelgrau 46 (2). The practice of units purchasing stocks of paint directly from commercial concerns was maintained and a list of suppliers accompanied HM Nr.864.

The pre-war orders may seem clear-cut but it would be unwise to assert that all German military vehicles without exception were painted in the Dunkelbraun 45 and Dunkelgrau 46 camouflage scheme during the 1940 campaign and indeed there are a number of genuine colour photographs, particularly of trucks and cars, proving that this was not so. Like many official orders, the July 1940 directive may have in fact sanctioned a practice which was already widespread. Interestingly, the opening sentence of HM Nr.864 states that the adoption of a single colour camouflage was intended to save paint.

In early 1941 the Wehrmacht was asked, at very short notice, to provide a mobile force to support the Italian army in North Africa and the first German units arrived in Libya in mid-February. It was very quickly realised that the dark grey camouflage of 1940 was completely counterproductive in the desert terrain in which the tanks and armoured cars were expected to operate. On 17 March 1941, HM Nr.281 introduced a new scheme utilising Gelbbraun RAL 8000, a rather dark yellow-brown, and a grey-green shade known as Graugrün RAL 7008. It was intended that RAL 8000 be the predominant colour, covering approximately two-thirds of the surface area and the edges where the two colours met were to be feathered. No time had been devoted to experimentation regarding the suitability of these colours and they were less than ideal but in plentiful supply. Both were in fact in use at the time by the Deutsche Reichsbahn which used Gelbbraun and Graugrün to paint railway cars and certain types of buildings respectively. Supplies of paint were to be obtained by the troops and, as with the previous orders, an extensive list of commercial suppliers was included in the body of the order. It should also be noted that HM Nr.281 does indeed describe RAL 8000 as Gelbbraun contrary to some accounts which suggest that the colour received its name at a later date. Replacement Pzkpfw III tanks, photographed at the port of Tripoli as early as April 1941, are clearly painted in these colours.

Operation Barbarossa, the invasion of the Soviet Union, commenced on 22 June 1941 and by that time it would be safe to assume that most, if not all, military vehicles which took part had been repainted in RAL 7021 Dunkelgrau (1).

This was a very dark neutral grey and although it tended to fade over time, genuine colour photographs of the period show that, when new, it is only marginally lighter than the black used for the Balkenkeuz. The single-colour camouflage remained in force until the winter months when, in most cases belatedly, whitewash

was issued to units in the field (2). As spring approached on the Eastern Front, HM Nr.315 of 25 March 1942 was issued which stipulated that the camouflage colours currently in use in North Africa were to be replaced by Braun RAL 8020, as a base coat, camouflaged with patches of Grau RAL 7027. The former was significantly lighter than Gelbbraun RAL 8000, which it superseded, and somewhat darker than our closest approximation of Dunkelgelb RAL 7028 which was introduced in 1943. The new colours were to be used only when existing stocks of RAL 8000 and RAL 7008 were exhausted and there is no way of knowing how gradual their introduction may have been. The Kassel plant of Henschel und Sohn, where the final assembly of the Tigers took place, may have had a supply of RAL 8000 and RAL 7008 as the company also produced the Pzkpfw III.

Officially at least no change had been introduced for those formations serving on the Eastern Front or stationed in western and central Europe although it had been realised for some time that the dark grey colour of the Panzers provided less than ideal camouflage on the open plains of Byelorussia and the Ukraine. It is clear that during the summer of 1942 there was widespread use of non-standard camouflage patterns, particularly among the units engaged in Fall Blau, the offensive aimed at securing the Caucasus oilfields.

This campaign, particularly its early stages, was covered extensively in German newsreels and magazines of the time and the many surviving colour photographs of armoured vehicles show that disruptive patterns in green and brown shades were applied to the Dunkelgrau base coat. It should be remembered that each order regarding changes in camouflage colours up to this time had stipulated that units were responsible for sourcing the necessary paint using their own funds and this would have allowed for a great deal of improvisation based on the appreciation of local conditions, limited only by the range of colours available (3).

In a complete break with the practice of using a dark grey base colour, HM Nr.181 of 18 February 1943 ordered that all vehicles were now to leave the factories and assembly plants in a colour described simply as dark yellow, or Dunkelgelb nach Muster, as no RAL number had been allocated at the time the order was issued. Units in the field were no longer to purchase supplies of paint and two camouflage colours, initially RLM Olivgrün (4) and Rotbraun RAL 8017, were supplied in the form of a paste in either 2-kilogram or 20-kilogram tins (5). It was not until 3 April 1943 that Dunkelgelb received the RAL code 7028 and the significance of this is that the colour could

Notes

1. The new classification for Dunkelgrau 46.

2. Although the use of whitewash was authorised by HM Nr.1128 dated 18 November 1941, it was some time before supply could meet demand and many units were forced to resort to expedients such as chalk and white sheets.

3. A list of colours available to army units, which probably accompanied one of the official orders, has survived the war although it is unfortunately undated. The inclusion of Braun RAL 8020 and Grau RAL 7027 would suggest that the list was compiled at some time after March 1942. A total of nineteen colours are listed including a range of greys and browns, Elfenbein RAL 1001, Beige RAL 1002 and Rotbraun RAL 8012 which was used as a primer.

4. The German air ministry, or Reichsluftministerium (RLM), maintained its own colour system. Why the army needed to resort to this source is unknown.

5. Rotbraun RAL 8017, also known as Schokoladenbraun, should not be confused with Rotbraun RAL 8012.

Notes

1. This vehicle is depicted on page 17 of the Camouflage & Markings section of this book.

2. A photograph of this vehicle and a profile illustration are shown on page 18.

3. *Tiger im Kampf,* published in English as *Tigers in Combat.* A tank of this battalion is depicted on page 22 of the Camouflage & Markings section of this book and the colours are also explained further.

not have been in use before February, as is often claimed, as it was a completely new shade. An interesting aspect of this order was the inclusion, for the first time, of a table indicating the exact amount of paint required, by weight, to paint certain types and classes of vehicle or weapon.

As the first Tiger I tanks were allocated to combat units in August 1942 it has generally been assumed, particularly by model manufacturers, that the Tigers issued to units serving on the Eastern Front in the period up to late February 1943 left the assembly plant painted in RAL 70212 Dunkelgrau. But there is good evidence that many were painted in the colours authorised for units serving in North Africa.

The difficulty in identifying these colours from monochrome photographs is compounded by the fact that most were covered in whitewash as soon as they arrived at the front and this would not have been removed until late March at the very least.

The initial production Tiger I tanks which were operated by 1.Kompanie, schwere Panzer-Abteilung 502 on the Leningrad Front in August 1942 were certainly painted in Dunkelgrau RAL 7021. This is confirmed by a very clear colour photograph of Tiger 100 which was captured intact by the Soviets and displayed in Moscow after its coat of whitewash had been carefully removed (1).

The nine tanks which were delivered to the battalion's 2.Kompanie in December 1942 appear to have been painted in RAL 7021 and, as mentioned in the chart on pages

62-3, their date of manufacture could have been at some time prior to November. At least one of the seven Tigers delivered in February 1943 shows signs of a third light colour and this could be Braun RAL 8020 or Gelbbraun RAL 8000 (2).

The tanks allocated to schwere Panzer-Abteilung 501 in September and October 1942 were photographed in Italy as they were loaded for shipping to Tunisia and are certainly finished in the North African colours. But there is strong evidence that some of these left the factory painted in Dunkelgrau and were repainted by the unit before they left Germany. This isexplored in some detail in *TankCraft 10: Tiger I, German Army Heavy Tank Southern Front North Africa, Sicily and Italy 1942-1945.*

In his three-volume study of the Tiger battalions (3), Oberst Wolfgang Schneider states that the Tiger I tanks shipped to schwere Panzer-Abteilung 503 were 'modified for hot-climate employment' in mid-November 1942 but refitted for deployment to the Eastern Front less than a month later on 16 December. This could refer to the fitting of the Fiefel air filter system, which was not a standard fixture before November, and its later removal. But if some of the tanks were also repainted it could explain the vastly different shades visible in monochrome photographs of the tanks of this battalion.

In *Germany's Tiger Tanks D.W. to Tiger I: Design, Production & Modification,* acknowledged experts Tom Jentz and Hilary Doyle state that tanks destined for

Although this photograph is of mediocre quality I have included it here as it is one of the few surviving images showing an initial production Tiger I of 1.Kompanie, schwere Panzer-Abteilung 502 without whitewash camouflage. These tanks are known to have been painted in Dunkelgrau RAL 7021 before leaving the Henschel factory and it can be seen here how quickly this colour became dull and faded. This vehicle, Tiger 111, is also shown on page 19 of the Camouflage & Markings section.

southern Russia' were designated as 'Tropen', or tropical, and painted in the North African camouflage scheme. They give the colours as Braun RAL 8020 and Grau RAL 7027 and they specifically mention that these colours were applied to the tanks allocated to Panzer-Regiment Grossdeutschland, SS-Panzer-Regiment 1, SS-Panzer-Regiment 2 and SS-Panzer-Regiment 3 between December 1942 and February 1943, a total of thirty-eight tanks. As the authors had access to the surviving archives of Henschel und Sohn these statements should be taken seriously. But their use of the term 'Tropen' has given rise to any number of theories explaining the use of colours other than Dunkelgrau RAL 7021 during 1942, most of them fanciful (1).

The terrain and weather of what is today southern Ukraine, Georgia and Azerbaijan is little different to that of the central front, although mountainous in parts, and cannot be compared to Libya or even Tunisia. Other than the units listed here by Jentz and Doyle, schwere Panzer-Abteilungen 502, 503, 504 and 505 received tanks in the period in question. The first two are dealt with above and the last is known to have had Tigers on hand as late as July 1943 which retained parts of a North Africa camouflage scheme (2). The thirty-two tanks of schwere Panzer-Abteilung 504, allocated in early 1943, were destined for service in Tunisia and were certainly painted in a base coat of either Braun RAL 8020 or Gelbbraun RAL 8000. As mentioned earlier, the Henschel plant probably had supplies of both. But if

RAL 7021 Dunkelgrau was still in use until mid-February 1943, as is generally supposed, the logistical problems of matching different colours to what units may have operated the vehicles in the East at some future date are obvious. For example, it was initially planned that 2.Kompanie of schwere Panzer-Abteilung 502 would support 1.Kompanie in the fighting around Leningrad when the tanks finally arrived in the East. But they were diverted, almost at the last minute, to southern Ukraine, the supposed 'Tropen' zone.

What should be remembered is that Henschel und Sohn was a commercial enterprise whose sole concern was developing and subsequently mass producing a commodity, thereby profiting the company. The priority of OKH, the army's high command, was to get as many Tigers into front-line service as quickly as possible and the question of which colour they were finished in was surely a secondary consideration. Indeed, the orders of late 1944 which introduced the factory-applied camouflage schemes stressed that supplies of vehicles to combat units were not to be held up due to shortages of officially sanctioned paint (3).

Given this, I believe that it is likely that the North African colours were incorporated into the general assembly process at some time in late November or early December 1942, with Dunkelgrau being used if necessary, and the use of these brown and green shades was one step along the road that led to the adoption of Dunkelgelb as a standard base coat in mid-1943.

Notes

1. The phrases given here in quotation marks are those used by Jentz and Doyle and it should perhaps be mentioned that the term 'Tropen', which has since passed into general usage when referring to these camouflage schemes, is not encountered in the original orders. In fact, the theatre of operations, North Africa, is stated specifically.

2. Schneider mentions that 3.Kompanie, schwere Panzer-Abteilungen 505 arrived at the front on 8 July 1943 painted in what he refers to as 'tropical markings' at a time when the fighting in Tunisia had been over for two months. This is explained in *TankCraft 20: Tiger I, German Army Heavy Tank Eastern Front, Summer 1943*.

3. The factory-applied schemes and colours are examined in detail in *TankCraft 13: Tiger I & Tiger II Tanks, German Army and Waffen-SS, The Last Battles in the West 1944-1945*.

An early production Tiger I of 13.Kompanie, Panzer-Regiment Grossdeutschland photographed at the time of the German offensive to recapture Kharkov in February 1943. Although the company's tanks are often portrayed in Dunkelgrau RAL 7021 they are known to have been painted in the North African camouflage colours of Braun RAL 8020 and Grau RAL 7027 as mentioned in the text. The contrast between these two shades is impossible to discern in monochrome photographs but at least one colour image shows that both were applied. Unlike most units on the Eastern Front at this time this company never employed whitewash camouflage.

TIGER I PRODUCTION AND ALLOCATION APRIL 1942-FEBRUARY 1943

Date	Production		Accepted	Fgst Nr	Allocated
	Planned	Achieved			
April 1942	1	1	0	V1	Heereswaffenamt
May 1942	3	1	1	250001 (1)	Heereswaffenamt
June 1942	5	0	0		
July 1942	10	0	0		
August 1942	10	8	8	250002 - 250009	schwere Panzer-Abteilung 502
September 1942	15	3	3	250010 - 250012	schwere Panzer-Abteilung 502
					schwere Panzer-Abteilung 501
October 1942	16	11	10	250013 - 250021 and V2	schwere Panzer-Abteilung 501
November 1942	18	25	17	250022 - 250038	schwere Panzer-Abteilung 501
					schwere Panzer-Abteilung 503
December 1942	30	30	38	250039 - 250076	schwere Panzer-Abteilung 503
					schwere Panzer-Abteilung 502
					SS-Panzer-Regiment 1
					SS-Panzer-Regiment 2
					SS-Panzer-Regiment 1
					schwere Panzer-Abteilung 501
January 1943 (7)	30	35	35	250077 - 250111 and V3	Heereswaffenamt
					schwere Panzer-Abteilung 502
					SS-Panzer-Regiment 1
					SS-Panzer-Regiment 2
					SS-Panzer-Regiment 3
					Panzer-Regiment Grossdeutschland
February 1943 (10)	30	32	32	250112 - 250143	Heereswaffenamt
					Panzer-Regiment Grossdeutschland
					schwere Panzer-Abteilung 501
					schwere Panzer-Abteilung 502
					schwere Panzer-Abteilung 504
					schwere Panzer-Abteilung 505
Totals		146	145 (11)		

All tanks were identified by a Fahrgestellenummer (Fgst Nr.), or chassis number and those of the Tiger I programme began with Fgst Nr. 250001, the first production vehicle, and ended with 251346 which left the assembly line in August 1944. The vehicles numbered V1, V2 and V3 were the experimental prototypes or Versuchs-Serie vehicles.

It should be borne in mind that the 250000 series of numbers was also, somewhat confusingly, used for the bare metal turret, the finished turret and the basic hull as well as the completed assembly. Surviving vehicles show that all these numbers were invariably different. For example, the Tiger I on display at the Bovington Tank Museum has turret number 250139 and hull number 250122. This is not evidence of extensive repair or cannibalism but rather the product of a system which identified a vehicle production programme by an allocated series number, in this case 250000, which was used by all the component manufacturers to identify their parts.

The bare metal hulls were built by either Krupp AG or Dortmund-Hoerder Hüttenverein (DHH) and an identifying number in the 250000 series was stamped on the outside of the turret roof. The number was followed by a three-letter code, either 'bwn' or 'amp', which identified Krupp or DHH respectively. The basic hulls, with suspension and most internal parts, were treated in a similar fashion, with the number stamped on the upper deck, usually near the driver's hatch. The turrets were completed by Wegmann & Co., and that company's 250000 serial number, followed by the letters 'cvd', was stamped inside the turret. In addition, the company's name, the serial number and date were inscribed on a metal plate that was fixed to the interior near the turret ring towards the front. The turret was delivered to Henschel where the final assembly took place and another number in the 250000 series, followed by the letters 'dkr' which denoted Henschel, and the last two numbers of the year, was stamped inside the hull on the driver's side. This is the true Fahrgestellenummer. The Wegmann and Henschel information was combined on a metal plate that was fixed to the driver's instrument panel. This plate also contained a Waffenamt acceptance stamp.

As the Fahrgestellenummeren shown in our chart in regard to production figures were taken from the records of Henschel und Sohn, the main assembly plant, we can assume that they refer to the finished vehicle.

Note that no mention is made in the allocation list exists for Fgst Nr.250002 to 250012, 250022, 250025 to 250027, 250034, 250081, 250091, 250093, 250097, 250101 to 250103, 250105, 2501017, 250113 to 250116, 250118 to 250121. From the February production run featured here, Fgst Nr. 2501127 to 250143, 250137, 250139 and 250143 were shipped to units in March 1943.

It should be mentioned that prior to May 1943 the records are incomplete, particularly as regards vehicle allocations, and our chart has been compiled from what information is available.

TIGER I PRODUCTION AND ALLOCATION APRIL 1942-FEBRUARY 1943

Quantity	Arrived	Fgst Nr	Production Batch
1	April 1942	V1	April 1942
1	May 1942	250001	June 1942
6	August 1942	250002 - 250007 (2)	August 1942
2	September 1942	250008, 250009 (2)	August 1942
1	September 1942	250010 (2)	September 1942
2	September 1942	250011, 250012 (3)	September 1942
8	October 1942	250013 - 250020	October 1942
10	November 1942	250021	October 1942
		250023, 250024, 250028, 250031 - 250033	November 1942
		250035 - 250038 (4)	November 1942
4	November 1942	Unknown (5)	
16	December 1942	250045, 250046, 250050, 250065	December 1942
9	21-28 December 1942	Unknown (6)	
1	December 1942	250053	December 1942
2	December 1942	250049	December 1942
5	December 1942	250048, 250066 - 250068	December 1942
1	9 December 1942	250059	December 1942
1	January 1943 (8)	V3	January 1943
3	5 February 1943	Unknown	
4	January 1943	250071 - 250073, 250075 (9)	December 1942
8	January 1943	250076 (9)	December 1942
		250077 - 250078, 250083 - 250086, 250088, 250092 (9)	January 1943
9	January 1943	250079, 250080, 250089, 250094 - 250096, 250101 - 250103 (9)	January 1943
7	February 1943	250082, 250087, 250090, 250098 - 250100, 250104 (9)	January 1943
1	February 1943	V2	October 1942
2	February 1943	250106, 250108 (9)	January 1943
2	5 March 1943	Unknown	
4	20 February 1943	Unknown	
20	February 1943	250109, 250111	January 1943
		250112, 250117 and 250122 - 250126	February 1943
2	February 1943	Unknown	
132			

1. Tiger Fgst Nr.250001, although often referred to as the first production vehicle, was delivered to the proving grounds at Kummersdorf on 17 May 1942 without a turret. It may have been fitted with a turret at some time in the following June, as one was requested from Krupp, but I have not been able to confirm this.

2. The Fahrgestellenummeren given by Oberst Schneider regarding these shipments cannot possibly be correct as they refer to November production vehicles. The numbers given here are taken from the battalion's diary as recorded in Tiger I & II: Kampf und Taktik by Thomas L. Jentz.

3. These numbers are somewhat speculative on my part but there were the only completed tanks available at that time.

4. Schneider mentions these tanks as allocated in August 1942 but they may have been shipped in November as shown here.

5. These tanks may have been 250022, 250025, 250026 and 250027 which were assembled in the first half of November and are not mentioned elsewhere

6. Oberst Schneider gives a figure of thirty-eight tanks delivered during December with eleven recorded Fahrgestellenummeren which leaves twenty-seven numbers unaccounted for while only twenty-five tanks were available. Numbers not mentioned as delivered in his list for the November and December production runs, besides those mentioned in note 5, are 250029, 250030, 250034, 250039 to 250044, 250047, 250051, 250052, 250054 to 250058, 250060 to 250064, 250069, 250070 and 250074. It may be that the deliveries to SS-Panzer-Regiment 1 and SS-Panzer-Regiment 2 were each short by one vehicle as suggested by Fahrgestellenummeren given here.

7. A total of thirty vehicles were delivered to operational units in January 1943, one of which was a rebuild.

8. The delivery date of December 1942 given in some sources cannot be correct as the V3 prototype was not completed until January 1943.

9. Jentz and Doyle are adamant that these tanks were finished in Braun RAL 8020 and Grau RAL 7027, the so-called Tropen scheme, as opposed to Dunkelgrau RAL 7021. This is discussed further in the text.

10. A total of thirty tanks were allocated to operational units during February, in addition to the V2 prototype, but it is likely that just eighteen, or at the most twenty-eight, were from the February production run.

11. This figure includes Fgst Nr.250001.

Dragon Models Ltd
B1-10/F., 603-609 Castle Peak Rd,
Kong Nam Industrial Building,
Tsuen Wan, N. T., Hong Kong
www.dragon-models.com

Tamiya Inc
Shizuoka City, Japan
www.tamiya.com

Trumpeter/Hobby Boss
NanLong Industrial Park, SanXiang,
Zhong Shan, GuangDong, P.R.China
www.trumpeter-china.com
www.hobbyboss.com

Academy Plastic Models
521-1, Yonghyeon-dong, Uijeongbu-si,
Gyeonggi-do, Korea
www.academy.co.kr

Hobby Fan/ AFV Club
6F., No.183, Sec. 1, Datong Rd, Xizhi City,
Taipei County 221, Taiwan
www.hobbyfan.com

Royal Model
Via E. Montale, 19-95030 Pedara, Italy
www.royalmodel.com

Italeri S.p.A.
via Pradazzo 6/b,
40012 Calderara di Reno, Bologna, Italy
www.italeri.com

Takom
www.takom-world.com

Meng-Model
www.meng-model.com

R Model
Darryl Bedford alerted me to these highly
detailed individual track links but I have
been unable to confirm any contact details
although they are available from a number
of retailers.

Rye Field Models
www.ryefield-model.com
An almost non-existent website. I would
recommend one of the on-line retailers.

Hauler
Jan Sobotka,
Moravská 38, 620 00 Brno,
Czech Republic
www.hauler.cz

Voyager
Room 501, No.411 4th Village,
SPC Jinshan District, Shanghai 200540,
P.R.China
www.voyagermodel.com

Griffon Model
Suite 501, Bldg 01, 418 Middle Longpan Rd,
Nanjing, P.R.China
www.griffonmodel.com

Aber
ul. Jalowcowa 15, 40-750 Katowice, Poland
www.aber.net.pl

E.T. Model
www.etmodeller.com

Friulmodel
H 8142. Urhida, Nefelejcs u. 2., Hungary
www.friulmodel.hu

Modelkasten
Chiyoda-ku Kanda, Nishiki-Cho 1-7, Tokyo,
Japan
www.modelkasten.com
Very difficult to navigate but worthwhile.

Theodoros Kalamatas Modelling Workshop
www.facebook.com/Theodoros-Kalamatas-
Modelling-Workshop

Eduard Model Accessories
Mirova 170, 435 21 Obrnice,
Czech Republic
www.eduard.com

Master Club
www.masterclub.ru
It appears that this firm is closely associated
with Armour35, a Russsian mail-order firm.

Model Artisan Mori
Yasutsugu Mori,
Maison Suiryu 302, Kunoshiro-cho 1-10,
Yokkaichi-City, Mie 510-0072, Japan
www.artisanmori.web.fc2.com

Model Factory Hiro
Yubinbango 121-0063 Adachi-ku, Tokyo,
Higashihokima 2-Chome, 3-8 Japan
www.modelfactoryhiro.com

RB Model
Powstancow Wlkp.29B,
64-360 Zbaszyn,
Poland
www.rbmodel.com

M Workshop Singapore
91 Bencoolen St, Sunshine Plaza 01-58,
Singapore
www.themworkshop.com

Zvezda (Zvezda-America)
www.zvezda-usa.com
Note that the Russian catalogue is not the
same as the US version.

ROCHM Model
www.rochmmodel.com
rochmmodel@gmail.com
This company has a huge selection of parts
and accessories for 1/35 scale Tiger models.

Throughout this series I have endeavoured to give the reader an understanding of the development a complex technical subject in a historical context while also providing the modeller with the inspiration to create a scale representation of what are arguably the most famous armoured fighting vehicles to take to the battlefield. In researching this project I consulted a number of works but no book on the Tiger I tank could be written without reference to *Germany's Tiger Tanks, DW to Tiger I: Design, Production & Modifications* by Hilary L. Doyle and the late Thomas L. Jentz. Although somewhat dated this work is the benchmark by which all other studies on this vehicle should be measured. I also drew heavily on the works of Oberst Wolfgang Schneider, particularly his histories of the Tiger battalions, and to a lesser extent the books of Horst Scheibert and Franz Kurowski. An invaluable resource are Thomas Jentz's Panzertruppen books which I would recommend to any reader with an interest in German armour of the Second World War period. I would very much like to acknowledge Hartmut von Holdt of Tiger im Focus for his many insightful observations, and the contributors to the Axis History and the Feldgrau forums, especially Martin Block and the late Ron Klages whose research on unit histories and vehicle allocations would fill many volumes. I would also like to thank the modellers who very generously allowed me to publish the images of their work. As always, I am indebted to Karl Berne, Valeri Polokov and J.Howard Parker for their invaluable assistance with the photographs and period insignia.

Tiger number 121 of 1.Kompanie, schwere Panzer-Abteilung 502 photographed just after it was captured by the Soviets. This tank is one of the first four that the company took to Russia in August 1942 and was also one of the first nine tanks to leave the assembly lines at Henschel. Note the Pzkpfw III stowage box fixed low on the turret rear in the manner which was common to the tanks of this company. The battalion's unit insignia is also just visible.